THE RIGHT  BLIC

Jointly by the same Authors

THE RIGHT WAY TO CONDUCT
MEETINGS, CONFERENCES AND
DISCUSSIONS

By H. M. Taylor and A. G. Mears

THE RIGHT WAY TO SPEAK IN PUBLIC

By
A. G. MEARS

*Gold Medalist, London Academy of Music (Public Speaking).
Gold Medalist, N.E.A. and Founder of the Abbey School for
Speakers, Westminster, London. Joint Author of the 'Right Way
to Conduct Meetings, Conferences and Discussions'.*

PAPERFRONTS

ELLIOT RIGHT WAY BOOKS
KINGSWOOD SURREY

Made and Printed in Great Britain by
Cox & Wyman Ltd., Reading.

PREFACE

I have revised this book and added two chapters dealing with words and phraseology in the hope that they will be helpful in enabling the beginner to grasp the natural working of the mind and the marvellous way in which feeling, ideas, knowledge, words and voice are integrated. Release of the mind from the bonds of inhibitions, conventions and mistaken loyalties is the crying need of this revolutionary age with its boundless possibilities and can only come with such knowledge.

People often wonder why a book was written. During the Second World War my son and his bomber crew were due to fly next day to Africa (on a journey from which they never returned) and our conversation ranged over many aspects of post-war reconstruction which these young men were pathetically determined should justify the insanity of war. What they so deplored was their inability ever to express their views vividly and constructively, in the right quarters. They lacked the know-how of public speaking. It was suggested that I should open a School for speakers and write a simple textbook on the subject. I have done so, I hope successfully, as a memorial to those few and for the benefit of the many.

> A People's voice! We are a people yet
> Tho' all men else their nobler dreams forget
> Confused by brainless mobs and lawless Powers;
> Thank Him who I'sled us here and roughly set
> His Briton in blown seas and stormy showers.
> We have a voice with which to pay the debt
> Of boundless love and reverence and regret
> To those great men who fought, and kept it ours —
> And kept it ours, O God, from brute control;
> O Statesmen, guard us, guard the eye the soul
> Of Europe, keep our noble England whole.
>   From "A People's Voice" (*Tennyson*)

A. G. MEARS.

CONTENTS

1

The Power of Speech and How to Develop it

Speech is the natural corollary of thought and perhaps the most poignant human tragedy is a creative mind frustrated by dumbness, sometimes self-imposed, sometimes the result of lack of education.

Imagine a fire burning fiercely behind a steel shutter, generating intense heat which must either set the chimney alight or burn itself out in dead, grey, lifeless ash. Imagine a similar process in the living tissues of the brain and you will get some idea of the terrifying results of mental frustration. No wonder that so many people shrink from the power of creative thought and never kindle the flame for fear of the disturbing consequences, without realizing that the ability to raise the shutter and release these vital, glowing thoughts, can be mastered. It is simply a matter of studying Nature's method of translating thoughts into words and so carrying the creative impulse to a satisfying conclusion.

You may ask yourself – can the expression of sincere thought in natural language be learnt? Certainly it can, provided the ideas are Sincere and the language Natural. The fallacy that speakers are born and not made arises from the disappointing results achieved by those who collect secondhand ideas, created by other, though probably greater, minds than their own, and then try to breathe life into these dry bones through the art of elocution. This method of artificial respiration may, through painstaking labour, revive life, but it is still secondhand life and the speaker will never acquire the dynamic power that springs naturally from harnessing reasoning powers and voice to creative ideas, ideas conceived and nurtured in the womb of a speaker's mind which search for the right word, the right gesture, the right appeal, searching always for the best presentation of this wonderful thought-child. The birth of a new idea is a great event and the driving force behind its desire for release is as powerful as a mother's love which works unceasingly to present the child of her creation to the world in the best possible light.

Recognition of these fundamental laws of Cause and Effect are the basis of the Right Way method. Speaking is recognized as a Science of the Mind, allied to the Art of Delivery, and its aim is to translate sincere feelings, by reasoning power, into natural speech.

The reader wishing to become a fluent speaker, is asked to accept the fact that feeling is the start of all natural speech or action and to realize that only fools speak when they have no ideas to convey. A simple sentence asking for a second helping at mealtime is the result of a feeling of unsatisfied hunger, the bold action of entering a shop and asking to see an article in the window is the result of a desire to own the article. In both cases feeling was the Cause and speech or action was the Effect, so it is natural that results are poor, when training in artificial Effects is tried, rather than attempts to diagnose and control the Causes, which would automatically produce the best results.

It is like trying to drive a car without starting up the engine, you may push it, or tow it, but it will only arrive under its own power if you use a self-starter. Feeling is the self-starter of natural speech and, before pressing it, the beginner should learn the component parts of the mental engine that is going to drive him to success, so that he can control them intelligently.

Analyse any good speech and you will find that roughly 50 per cent is subject matter, 20 per cent the psychology of approach and conclusion and 20 per cent effective delivery. This leaves only 10 per cent for personality, a small percentage it is true, but that 10 per cent is so powerful that it acts as leaven for the whole loaf. Readers must supply the 10 per cent personality themselves; but this should not be difficult, as speech training on these lines, if properly applied, cannot fail to develop personality. The remaining 90 per cent can be learned by careful study of the following chapters dealing with speech construction, effective notes and memory, overcoming nervousness, tuning in to audiences and finally, adequate delivery.

A speech falls naturally into three parts, the approach, the main facts, and the conclusion. The approach depends on quick and skilful tuning in, and good advice was once given to me when I was told "If you do not strike oil in three minutes, stop boring".

Many a good speech has been ruined by a dull, nervous beginning and more will be said on this subject in the appropriate chapter on psychology. Interest and attention must be aroused before reason responds and, once lost, is hard to regain.

The main section relies for success on expert pruning of words so that the facts stand out clearly and language is not debased by using words to cover a vacuum, to say nothing of the risk of being told you are intoxicated with the exuberance of your own verbosity.

The conclusion should be the spot-lighting of your main points by the unleashing of powerful emotion and the whole speech should be illumined by the personality of the speaker shining from the twin arc lamps of sincerity and knowledge.

Does this sound impossibly difficult or are you thinking that the standard of speaking envisaged in this chapter is too high? True, it is high, but it can be achieved, and the result is worth the effort. There is no short cut to success; good speaking is more a matter of perspiration than inspiration. It entails mental concentration of a high order, but mastery of the following chapters will give you a feeling of exhilaration through the realization of your own power and you will no longer be content to make secondhand speeches from secondhand material, however good. Rather will you practise creating speeches on many subjects for all occasions. Once you have created the shape of your future speech, your creative mind will then call on reason to fill in the outline with interesting material, and finally you will enjoy making attractive frames. You will be surprised how much more effectively you will speak when you have mastered the art of focusing points. You will only want to speak when prompted by the urgent need to convey an idea and your trained mind will reject superfluous words. A long-suffering public has endured the windbag for too long, and the type of speaker who does not know when he rises what he is *going to say*, has no idea what he *is saying* when on his feet and no idea what he *has said* when he sits down, will no longer be tolerated. This is an age of specialists and nobody should attempt public speaking without realizing the immense power of creative thought expressed through the medium of speech, and the need for expert handling of such a force.

On this note let us tackle together the task of studying a method which we hope will enable the reader, at any time, to drive to success, through the ability to release constructive ideas at the right moment and in the Right Way, to his own immeasurable benefit and, who knows, possibly to the benefit of a world sadly lacking in leadership. We will begin by outlining the whole course.

To continue the simile of a car, the engine of the mental car is obviously the first thing to construct and the component parts are feeling, which is the counterpart of fuel and ignition, and reason, which canalizes ideas, designs the engine, and filters the fuel. The next two chapters will help you to master the basic rules.

When you have constructed your engine and familiarized yourself with all its parts, you will need instruction in lubrication (Chapter 4) so that you can keep it in perfect working order and you will then be ready to create a body worthy of your engine. Your comfort and that of your hearers will depend on attractive presentation and framing of facts, and just as a car requires a strong frame, springs, padding and windows, so a speech requires repetition of points to hold arguments together, tactful presentation of controversial matter, and wise use of imagination and colouring. These essentials for building, colouring, and polishing the body of your speeches are often neglected by speakers who concentrate on facts to the exclusion of all else, so Chapters 5, 6, and 7 deal with them fully and readers are advised to study these chapters carefully.

Finally you have to learn to drive the car, and you must first study the causes of Nervousness, which is part of the creative impulse and should be welcomed rather than dreaded. To be nervous is to be sensitive and vital, so training in control and the use of nervousness, rather than any attempt to deaden it is given in Chapter 8.

When you have acquired reasonable nerve control you can venture on Delivery of your speech, and the wonderful mechanism of the voice can be tested. This miracle has been provided by Nature and should respond adequately to mind direction, so skill in using it is largely a matter of practice. Delivery is purposely left to the end of the training as you should not be voice conscious while speaking. It is more important to concentrate on *what* you are saying rather than how you are saying it, but you should know the function of the lungs, lips, teeth, tongue, jaw, and voice registers in order to check and eradicate any faults that may develop. Chapter 9 deals with Delivery, but it is only intended to check elementary faults, as voice production is a subject in itself with which I do not propose to deal in this book. If you use your voice correctly, it should serve to express sincere thought in the natural way, and should only need overhauling periodically. Mannerisms which distract both the speaker and the audience are also dealt with in that chapter.

The final chapter deals with finer points such as emphasis, phrasing, and the minor faults that tend to develop from time to time. The Appendix gives you quotations from famous speakers as the study of great orators and their methods teach many lessons. Do not envy them, but look up to them as travellers who have reached the top of the hill of success where you will soon join them. Why not? Everything must have a beginning and who knows the power of your speech until you have designed, built, and tested it.

These then are the lessons to be learned and you will realize that speech training, to be effective, is long and arduous, but if you are keen and prepared for hard work, you will find it fascinating and will never regret the time devoted to it.

2

Creative Ideas and Feeling

A speech falls naturally into three parts – the approach, the main facts and the peroration, and as subject matter is 50 per cent of the whole and the most important section, the handling of it must be the first stage of preparation.

Success depends on perfect harmony between feeling and reason, so preparation should start with your own conclusions and ideas, out of which you can sketch your outline and then call on reason to supply the facts.

How are you going to extract your own feelings and ideas? Here is where you start work in real earnest, so come into the workshop of Imagination and start developing your faculty of mental concentration. You will soon agree with me that public speaking is a matter of training and practice, and remember that overalls and backless benches are more suitable for workshops than fires and armchairs! Prepare your mind accordingly, retire to a room alone, sit up at a table with pencil and paper and devote an hour or two to hard work.

The first tool you will have to master is the pneumatic drill of mental concentration, which will enable you to break up the hard surface of vague thoughts which lie uppermost in your mind and which must be probed before you can extract the real creative thoughts underneath.

Most minds have a superficial crust of secondhand ideas, photographic impressions, undigested facts, headlines and slogans or worst of all, the imprints of propaganda. If this crust has been allowed to accumulate over years, and has never been probed by conscious, constructive thoughts, it will have become a rock-like barrier between the reasoning and the creative sections of your mind. The result is shallow, but often fertile, soil on the surface of the rock, teeming with rootless ideas and passing fancies, but underneath the rock, the creative soil is starved and barren, as it is receiving no nourishment and only the fortunate few can strike roots deep enough to create their own ideas, unaided by water from the general pool of knowledge on the surface. The majority of speeches spring from this shallow soil – note the average conversation and you will be surprised how often it starts from "I said to him" or "He said to me" or merely "They say." Again how often remarks revolve round the weather, the domestic scene, food problems, or the repetition of obvious facts bought for pence at the newsagents. All this is good enough for the small change of conversation, but is shoddy, secondhand material from which to build inspiring speeches.

This shallow soil is often the sole source of inspiration of the glib speaker who weaves words with great skill round unquestioned platitudes. No wonder he is unconvincing, though often attractive. How tired we get of his artificial rhetoric and endless repetition and how we long for an original idea, or even an interesting individual conclusion reached by the speaker after careful study of the facts; but, alas! such thoughts are stored in the creative mind and the spring which releases them is constructive thought, with which the speaker is unfamiliar. Unfortunately the undiscerning listener often labels such a speaker "a born orator", because he cannot distinguish between marionettes of thought, skilfully manoeuvred by the strings of good delivery and a good vocabulary, and real inspiration. Success of such a speaker can bring little satisfaction to his creative mind, rather will it lead to a sense of frustration which the speaker will probably attribute to the *futility of speech* rather than to *his own faulty methods* of preparation. Temporary success is often followed by disaster when the public has an opportunity of comparing such artificial efforts with the real orator, whether born or developed by training, who must essentially be a thinker first and a speaker afterwards, for so it has been decreed by Nature herself.

If this is the fate of the glib speaker, who can cover up the absence of constructive ideas attractively, how much worse off is the speaker who has not even mastered the art of delivery! He meets disaster right away, though too often it is unrecognized by him, owing to the courtesy and patience of the audience, and he is allowed to bore audiences indefinitely until he becomes a menace.

If any reader has encountered easy success through a natural skill with word spinning and is content, he need read no further, for this book is intended for those who wish to climb the heights, and who are prepared to put in immense efforts in order to master the art of creating a speech from original ideas.

To them I would say, analyse your mind, study the depth of the crust you have to penetrate and then get to work with your drill. The ease with which you penetrate to your creative mind depends on your knowledge of the subject you have chosen for your speech. Most people probe matters in which they are interested and if you have knowledge of the subject you will find it comparatively easy – as the essence of the matter will have been seeping into your mind for a considerable time – and you will have produced your ideas, and formed your conclusions, which will be sincere, natural and eager for release. That is why speaking on your own subject is easier and probably half an hour's mental concentration will extract the whole outline of your speech, even to the extent of main headings and sub-headings.

If for training purposes, however, you have wisely chosen a subject about which you have general impressions and vague ideas rather than expert knowledge, the task is more difficult. You will probably find that the thoughts you extract at random are of two kinds. The bulk of them will be conclusions you have unconsciously formed at various times as a result of constructive thought based on observations or acquired knowledge. The remainder will be original ideas which you have probably created in the process of forming your conclusions, and then pigeon-holed, waiting for conscious mental stimulus to give them life and expression. In addition you will conceive fresh thoughts as you go along, and these creative ideas are the gems which will scintillate and reflect your personality in the speech. The more original your mind and the more you have used your powers of imagination, the more you will enjoy producing your own ideas, but like Nature's creative method, the process may be painful and the labour long in the early stages, though it will become easier with practice – and it will be accompanied by an exhilarating feeling of achievement. Conclusions you can accept and check later, but ideas must be carefully sifted to extract the gold from the dross, a fascinating job which cannot be done hurriedly. Indisputably this is the most important stage of speech training and failure to realize its importance is one of the chief causes of lifeless speech.

Reason may suggest that the speech material you have extracted from your creative mind is flimsy and worthless, but reject such advice, as the creative mind treats reason as a subordinate to be called in later to supply facts, just as an artist creates a picture in his mind and then later selects suitable materials for transferring it to canvas. Remember Your Own thoughts are the only ones in which your creative mind is interested, *they* are the inspiration for your subject matter, the basis of good psychology and delivery, and the source of your effective personality. Every part of your speech depends on their dynamic power.

In the analysis of a good speech given in the previous chapter I suggested 10 per cent only for personality, but the inspiration of creative ideas colours the remaining 90 per cent. I tried, possibly unsuccessfully, as they are so interwoven, to differentiate the many physical attributes, which make up pure "personality" from the inspiration of creative ideas which vivify a speech and can emanate from a fine brain behind a colourless personality.

Some readers may question the low percentage allocated to personality in my analysis, and maintain, quite rightly, that a strong personality can carry a weak speech to success, and that therefore it is the prime factor in successful speaking. This is a widely held view, but it is a superficial one. A speech, unprepared, and coloured by personality alone, leaves an audience with vague impressions, and when the personality of the speaker has faded, they are lucky to retain even a smattering of the subject because they have allowed 10 per cent to obscure 90 per cent.

Personality should propel reason and not submerge it, and must be used as skilfully and sparingly as a chef uses flavouring. The latter is less than 10 per cent of his ingredients but the success of the whole dish may depend on it. I stress this point because too much reliance is often placed on personality and insufficient importance attached to the inspiration of creative ideas. The glib speaker relies on personality, but the dynamic speaker draws his strength from creative thought and feeling. To test the truth of this, recall instances of normally inarticulate people, with seemingly colourless personalities who speak surprisingly well in an argument when they feel compelled to refute a statement which has angered them. Anger was the magnet which extracted their creative thought, and this powerful force used reason, words, gestures, and voice instinctively to the best advantage. Spontaneous speech is often the finest expression of thought, because feeling has unconsciously pressed the self-starter of speech, but why wait for the accidental release of this power, when you can train yourself to control and release it at will.

The foundation of training in the workshop of imagination, is practice in stimulating interest by means of mental concentration and since "practice makes perfect" do the following exercise many times before passing on to the next stage of training. Choosing different subjects on different days, write down everything that occurs to you, whether it be conclusions previously reached, conclusions which emerge as the result of constructive thought, or inspiring ideas which will come to the lucky owners of an imaginative mind. Take easy and difficult subjects alternatively, *i.e.* when you merely want pleasant relaxation choose a subject with which you are familiar and you will find it easy to extract ideas previously formed through interests and knowledge, but do not be content with easy success.

When you are prepared to get down to hard work, choose a subject in which you are interested but know very little, and repeat the process of extracting ideas twice, allowing an interval of twenty-four hours or more between each attempt. Make your second list of ideas without reference to the first, then compare the two lists, and pick out those that recur, as they will be genuine conclusions that your mind has retained and you will be convinced of their soundness and will have no difficulty in remembering them, or presenting them in a convincing way, when delivering your speech. Other ideas are probably passing fancies which may or may not seem of value on second thoughts.

When you have done this exercise frequently you will have learnt to extract creative ideas on both familiar and less familiar subjects, but two warnings are offered to those who are tempted to try short cuts. Never work when your mind is tired, and do not be tempted to acquire material from outside sources at this stage, as you must learn to rely on yourself in the first instance.

The last and most difficult exercise in concentration is to extract material for a speech from a subject to which you have given *no* previous thought. You will not acquire the necessary self-confidence to speak on any subject with equal ease until you can do this, so try the following. Look round the room and select an object at random, concentrate until your observation suggests an idea, however trivial, and continue concentration until ten or twelve unrelated ideas have been jotted down. The following tables are an example of the sort of ideas which might occur to you if you chose a fire, or a chair – and in case you think they are hopeless material from which to build an interesting speech, I will help you to develop them from the initial stage to the final outline:

IDEAS

ILLUSTRATION 1. *Coal Fire*

1. Warm and Comfortable.
2. Makes work.
3. Smoky and dirty.
4. Extravagant.

So far it is easy as these are obvious conclusions based on experience, as you will feel warm – realize you have to do the grate and realize that a coal bill looms in the future! If your mind now pauses – start a train of thought by fixing your eyes on a lump of coal. In a few seconds, if concentrating you will ask yourself:

5. What is coal?
6. How do we get it?
7. Should we have open fires or gas or electric?
8. What is a coal mine like?
9. How do miners live?
10. How many miners are there?
11. Why is coal important?

This will lead to bigger issues, and if you have become interested you will start thinking about coal in relation to the power, industry and the Nation, and their attendant problems, which is a good wide note on which to finish, *i.e.* your last point.

12. National importance.

If latter too advanced stop at question 10.

ILLUSTRATION 2. *A Chair*

Observation will suggest that it has legs, seat, and a back, so your first thoughts might be:

1. Why does it have legs and a back?
2. Is it comfortable?
3. Why were chairs invented?
4. Different kinds of chairs.

Here your mind may pause so start a train of thought by considering the material. If upholstered this will suggest different kind of coverings, so your next points may be:

5. Different coverings.
6. Material – *i.e.* wood, metal, plastic.
7. Origin of materials.

This will bring you to the artistic angle and you may get:

8. Period chairs.
9. Craftsmanship.
10. Mass production.
11. Are chairs the right shape for comfort after all?
12. How would the absence of chairs affect our homes, our work, and our lives?

These two examples will show you the natural workings of the mind once started. Think of a stone thrown into a pond and the ever widening ripples reaching to the farthest shore. Your first idea is the stone and subsequent ideas the ripples, and the most unlikely subject tackled in this way will lead to amazing results.

This is the final stage of training before leaving the workshop of Imagination, and like the initial training in most professions, it is the most difficult as the ground covered is so unfamiliar. To the keen student, I would say, that patient application of these lessons will bring its own reward, as exploration of your own creative mind, possibly unexplored hitherto, is essential to success as a speaker. It may be a matter of days, weeks or months, according to the degree of training your mind has previously received and your ability to concentrate, but it is within the capacity of the average intelligence. You will not enjoy the self-confidence which comes from knowledge, until you can extract the outline of a speech from:

(a) a subject with which you are familar – the easiest test.

(b) a subject in which you are merely interested.

(c) a subject to which you have previously given no thought – the final test.

Does this seem too long, arduous and difficult a training, and are you doubtful of its necessity? Well, the Right Way holds out no promise of easy success and you were warned that the hill was steep, and if the propelling power is inadequate you will never reach the summit. Remember the wise saying that "Genius is the capacity for taking great pains", and the patience and perseverance brought to bear on sharpening your mental tools will bring wonderful results for it will enhance your personality, sharpen your wits, improve your observation, and colour your whole life – assets of great worth whether applied to speech-making or in any other walk of life.

You have now learned that mental concentration is the first and most important tool in the fashioning of a speech and must be mastered, however difficult. You will also realize that the only material worthy of such a tool is *your own creative ideas*. Do not be despondent if your material seems unworthy of your efforts, remember that "the greatest unexplored territory lies under your own hat" and that ideas produce further ideas once your interest has been stimulated.

It is this interest which will urge you to take the next step into the Workshop of Reason where you will learn the rules of architecture so that your tools can be effectively used.

3

Construction

The Workshop of Reason

Feeling and creative thought, to be effective, must now be harnessed to reason, which is the next stage of training. Here you will learn to canalize ideas, plan, design, and check your facts, as well as acquiring additional information.

The first impression you will receive in this Workshop of Reason is one of calm methodical orderliness, and you will welcome the familiar tools of applied reason and acquired knowledge, which you have learnt to handle at school and in your work. This peaceful atmosphere, and the willing help available from many sources, will be very restful after the undisciplined turbulence of the creative mind and the frightening isolation of individual thoughts. The restlessness of the pneumatic drill gives way to the quieter tools of applied reason and research, and fashioning of your raw material into a finished speech becomes increasingly interesting. No doubt artists and novelists feel the same sense of relief when their ideas are stabilized, and the transference of them to canvas or paper is merely a matter of treatment and skill.

Mental concentration is still necessary, but you are not handling high explosive, and you can proceed at your own pace. Gone is the overwhelming sense of urgency which the creative impulse brings forth, and the fear that your creative ideas are non-existent, imagination dead and your mind a blank. You have discovered that you can start your engine by mental concentration, generate sparks through feeling, and that the fuel of ideas *is* available, so you must now learn to construct a map so that you can be sure of using your engine to reach your destination without anxiety. Let us start by canalizing ideas and planning design which is a craftsman's job, governed by definite rules which we will now consider.

Canalizing Ideas.

The first lesson Reason teaches is to separate your random thoughts into groups, each with an appropriate title which will form the main headings of your speech. This is to train your mind to consider one group of ideas at a time, and is designed to prevent rambling vagueness and irrelevance. In the workshop of Imagination you were allowed to work *how* you liked, *when* you liked and *as* you liked, to flit from idea to idea, extracting as much or as little as fancy prompted. The result was probably a jumble of creative ideas and constructive conclusions in hopeless confusion, and at intervals you shook up this kaleidoscope of thought and hoped that the fragments would form an attractive pattern.

Many minds never follow a train of thought to the end, and merely toy with ideas like children attracted by pretty colours. Training methods in the workshop of Reason are very different, the whole aim being to harness the natural creative mind, and use it as the motive power to achieve practical ends. Just as the first step in breaking in horses is to accustom them to a leading rein, so you must canalize your ideas and drive them quietly and patiently, but inexorably, to a given point, however many times they try to break away. The stronger the creative mind, the harder the breaking-in process, but imagination and reason must work together to connect thought with feeling for practical purposes.

Of course, a free, unfettered, creative mind, with no conscious reference to reason, can and does produce masterpieces which we rightly attribute to pure inspiration, but this is more usual when the purpose is to provide food for the soul rather than the mind. Most musicians, artists, actors, writers, and speakers, however, master the technique of their trade, and work through recognized channels.

In the case of writers and speakers, the more practical the object of the article or speech, the more reason should be called in to help. Many readers of this book will require the power of speech for practical purposes, and will therefore recognize the importance of driving the propelling power of creative thought to the desired end by means of reason. Here you have the secret of the seeming disharmony between the creative and the practical mind, and the origin of the saying, "Speakers are born and not made". They are "born" *and* "made" and the speaker who works to a practical plan through reason while leaving his creative mind free to bring in fresh ideas, illustrations and inspiration, is following Nature's method of the bee, the beaver or the bird. Note the perfect combination of the animals who build the honeycomb, the dam, or the nest on orthodox lines, and those who bring in all kinds of new material, hoping that it can be used to achieve the perfection which is the aim of all.

Ability to group ideas is the next lesson to be mastered, and it is best to begin with an easy subject with plenty of obvious ideas which you can use as material to be planned. Try "The Uses of Electricity", write down everything you know that is run by electricity, then put against each item the appropriate main heading, and those main headings will form the first section of the pipe through which you direct your thoughts. The result may be something on these lines:

IDEAS	MAIN HEADINGS
1. Hoover.	1. Domestic.
2. Cooker.	2. Domestic.
3. Lift.	3. Transport.
4. Radio.	4. Communication.
5. X-ray.	5. Medical.
6. Iron.	6. Domestic.
7. Dynamo.	7. Industry.
8. Kidney Machine.	8. Medical.
9. Trains.	9. Transport.

Very little thought will suggest a hundred uses, but the method is the same, jot them down at random and attach a main heading to each one.

Planning Design

Now decide the order of your main points, as you will want a logical sequence, and a design of your own creation. You will be less likely to forget any section when delivering the speech, if you are interested in the weaving of your own pattern.

Everybody has their own method, but I find it helpful to start from the point most likely to appeal to the majority of my hearers, and work outwards from that point on a plan of my own. In this case for instance – I would take the Domestic angle first, if speaking to women, and focus my mind on this section only and plan the development. I might take a tour of the house starting with the door bell and working through all the rooms, noting every electric gadget, or alternatively I might take food, lighting, heating, and personal comfort as sub-headings. I would prepare *each section* in the same way and might decide to take my main points in the following order:

1. Domestic.
2. Transport.
3. Industry.
4. Communication.
5. Medical

I would then need some link between points, and connection of ideas might suggest a train on leaving the house (Transport) a visit to a factory (Industry), an accident to bring in telephoning for the doctor (Communications), and an X-ray (Medical).

Does this sound too fanciful? Believe me it is a very reliable method, as one idea will naturally lead to the next, and you can keep the fairy tale as a mental guide if you think it sounds too childish to be woven into a serious speech. If this method does not appeal to you – do not attempt it – the important point is that ideas must run in logical sequence, or your speech will be jerky and disconnected. When dealing with the past, present, and future, place them in that order – if your subjects affect both individuals and nations, work your design from the personal to the district, and on to the nation and finally to the world, or the reverse order. It is surprising how many speakers ignore this golden rule through lack of preliminary preparation.

I once heard a well-known speaker dealing with Social

Services, tell his audience that we are cared for from the cradle to the grave. The subsequent talk, however, took us through Education, Old Age Pensions, Maternity and Child Welfare, and finished with Social Security. Any logical mind, listening to such a speech, would feel irritated and the confusion in the speaker's mind would communicate itself to the minds of the audience.

Working on methodical lines, you will soon learn to design the whole speech, which will have been conceived by your creative mind and fashioned by reason. Standard designs can be used again and again, either for a composite speech on a big subject, or each section can be expanded into a simple talk, which saves a vast amount of future preparation, and is invaluable to a busy speaker.

Having reached this stage you should experience a satisfactory feeling of real progress, something tangible is emerging at last. Possibly you are thinking how presumptuous it is for speakers to imagine they are equipped to face audiences without any preliminary training, and how small is their chance of success! You will have realized that more is required from a speaker than a good brain and voice. It is a Science of the Mind, allied to the Art of Delivery, and until this is recognized by the educational authorities, the standard of public speaking in this country will continue to be deplorable.

Before you leave the planning section try out the rules of design on the ideas which you extracted on Coal Fires and Chairs when exploring the creative mind. Results might be as follows:

COAL FIRES

MAIN IDEAS | SUB-HEADINGS

1. *Practical thoughts*

(a) Warm and comfortable.
(b) Smoky and dirty.
(c) Makes work.
(d) Extravagant.
(coal bill links with next section).

MAIN IDEAS	SUB-HEADING

2. *The Coal Industry*
  (a) What is coal?
  (b) How do we get it?
  (c) Conditions in mines.
  (d) Miners lives.

3. *National importance of coal*
  (a) Size of industry.
  (b) Basis of electricity generation.
  (c) Value of by-products.
  (d) Its use in industry.

(Frame for a speech – see chapter 5.)

CHAIRS

1. *Random thoughts on chairs*
  (a) Why were chairs invented?
  (b) Origin of legs and back.
  (c) Comfort versus utility.
  (d) Different types for different purposes.

2. *History of chairs*
  (a) Material, *i.e.* wood, metal, plastic.
  (b) Coverings.
  (c) Craftsmanship.
  (d) Examples of period chairs.

3. *Future of chairs*
  (a) Utility versus craftsmanship.
  (b) Price.
  (c) Mass production methods and design.
  (d) Employment.

4. *New ideas*
  (a) Are chairs designed for comfort?
  (b) Effect of no chairs – on home, work, and life.

(Frame for above speech – see Chapter 5)

Here then is your design, and though you would probably develop it differently according to the degree of interest you feel in the various ideas, the lesson learnt will be the same. You will now realize that by mental concentration you can build an interesting speech on any subject, if you start from some focal point, which can be either an idea, or the photographic impression of an object which you observe, provided it is worked out on sound rules for design. You will then be ready for the third stage of training.

Mapping your route

Canalizing ideas and planning the design corresponds to the construction of a reliable map which should be followed if you are to speak with ease and certainty as this will satisfy your creative mind that ideas will reach their destination and reason that they will get there by the most direct route, then you can consider if those ideas have sufficient driving force to complete the journey.

Remember these thoughts were either original, or based on knowledge which has seeped through from the surface impressions, and the latter may have been inaccurate at its source. Your creative mind has not questioned its accuracy, it merely seized on points of interest from which to construct ideas, but reason warns you that though this may be good enough for your own thoughts or for conversation, it is highly dangerous on a platform if unchecked. Any doubts as to the accuracy of what you are saying will rightly arouse in your mind the bogy of the all-knowing questioner in the audience – the cause of so much nervousness. This doubt as to accuracy will occur to you just as you are about to express your point, and will cut across your train of thought, and stop the flow of words. To avoid this you must check your facts. Ideas which have been adequately checked are given out convincingly, the voice gains strength and colour, and you welcome rather than dread a questioner when you know you have the *Encyclopaedia Britannica* at your back. Checking is a simple matter, but in the course of it you will probably realize that you have insufficient ideas and knowledge to do justice to your subject, so now for the *first time* you go to other sources for information, and we will leave the analogy of the engine which was only intended to explain the mechanism of the mind behind speech construction.

Acquiring knowledge

Having decided on your main ideas you will simplify your search for knowledge and you will thoroughly enjoy browsing leisurely in libraries, or visiting various sources of information from which to collect the facts you need to strengthen and colour your speech.

Many speakers start their speech preparation at this stage, thus by-passing creative thought and building their speech from reason alone. This is obviously better than the glib speaker who relies on words and impressions, but at best it is dead, lifeless, speech, as secondhand ideas, however good, will never engender the dynamic power of the creative mind.

The chief point to remember in collecting additional facts, is that they must fit into your own design, and amplify your own thesis, so once more reason insists that you work to a plan.

Take each section of your speech in turn and collect facts relevant to your sub-headings. Do not bring in a fresh group of ideas, or you will unbalance the whole design, and your creative mind will lose interest, as it will only welcome matter to strengthen its own ideas. Regulate the amount of information to the time allotted to your speech, but keep additional facts in reserve to fill up gaps. Acquiring the necessary knowledge should increase the interest and enthusiasm already generated in your mind for a speech of your own creation which now has some substance as well as a clear design, and you should want to try it out. Trust yourself to find words and voice naturally. Remember that you cannot learn to *speak* in public by *thinking* or *writing* speeches. You must now practise quick co-ordination of ideas, words and voice which occurs automatically in conversation. The best practice is to familiarize yourself with the route to be followed by trying a short, five-minute speech, confining yourself to main points without amplification. Do this several times, using different words, but check facts to prevent rambling. Changing the order in which you deal with points each time shows lack of self-control and leads to disharmony between your creative and reasoned mind. It also makes your map a hindrance rather than a help.

Start your speech by repeating your main points firmly to give your mind clear direction, then take each section and develop the subheadings, and at the end repeat your main points again, as repetition is essential in speaking, one of the main differences between the technique of speech and the technique of writing. There is a lot of sound sense in the remark of one of Lewis Carroll's characters – "When I say a thing *three* times it is true". The natural reaction of an audience to something they do not know is that it cannot be true, the second time they hear it they remember it vaguely without realizing that you have just told them, and the third time you repeat it, they are convinced that they knew it before you. In a five-minute speech the repetition is obvious, but it is good mind training nevertheless, as the outlining of points at the beginning of your main section gives your mind clear direction, repetition as you deal with each point keeps you from rambling, and the repetition at the end, before your conclusion, reminds hearers of your main points. In a full-length speech this repetition is even more necessary and is not noticeable. This is only a suggestion, and not a rule, as the fewer the rules the better. In time and with experience you will develop your own style. Some subjects such as travel-talks do not lend themselves to rigid outlines, though you still need outlines in the background.

Have you passed your first test satisfactorily? If so, your patient study will have been rewarded, as the ability to link feeling and reason is the acid test of good speaking, and a power of which you have little conception. Hitler and Mussolini discovered it and used it for evil. Churchill and Roosevelt used it for good, but all four realized that the emotional appeal must precede the appeal to reason, and having unleashed this powerful force, they then used it for their own ends. We all know the power of unspoken thought on those around us – mobilize that power through the channels of speech, as nature intended us to do, and so fulfil your destiny.

When you first try out your speech you will be inexperienced and may be disappointed – but do not despair, rather examine your lubrication system, and see if that is at fault. This is a matter of notes and memory so we will deal with them in the next chapter.

4

Notes and Memory
for Lubrication

By this time you have learnt to link the creative with the reasoned mind, and will have realized their interdependence.

Remember, however, that they are sometimes hostile, and usually suspicious of each other, and a sound lubrication system is necessary to ensure smooth working and co-ordination.

Reason will rely on notes to recall facts, and feeling will rely on memory to recall its own creative ideas, so your oil must consist of reliable notes and a well-trained memory.

NOTES

If you have trained your mind in the Right Way – notes will present no difficulties, as you are working on Ideas, and have never confused the issue by writing out sentences. To do so, is to court disaster, as all the unimportant words will catch your eye, and you will have to pause and search for the idea, and so break your train of thought and your contact with the audience. Alternatively you may patter on in a vague futile way, using words to cover the pause, while you are trying to focus the next point. This is even more disastrous, as a pause would at least give your audience a chance to relax, but why break the friendly contact when your mind should be able to collect the next idea by a hasty glance at your notes, if the *Ideas* stand out in bold lettering, conveyed by single words if possible, never by long sentences.

Confine your notes to Main Headings, numbered numerically, with sub-headings, numbered alphabetically. Never pack many ideas into a small space by means of minute writing, or you will not be able to read them and they will irritate rather than help. Remember amenities for speakers are usually absent, tables are low, and Chairmen rarely think of placing a pile of books or a box on their right, to bring the speaker's notes up to a convenient level. The result is that you have to glance down a long way, probably the lighting is poor, and as your mind is always ahead of your tongue, you will be delivering your last sentence while your mind is focusing the next point. This dual task will cause your mind to react more slowly and it will take a fraction longer than usual to grasp an idea, so you must make sure that the ideas are conveyed in the quickest and easiest manner.

If speaking on Agriculture – your notes might be as follows: —

A POLICY FOR RURAL ENGLAND

1. INDIVIDUAL FARMS.

   (a) Crops. Fertilizers.
   (b) Labour. Wages.
   (c) Marketing – prices.

2. NATIONAL PLAN.

   (a) State. Control or guidance?
   (b) Rural industries.
   (c) Rural amenities.

3. WORLD ASPECT OF AGRICULTURE.

   (a) Link between nations.
   (b) Basis of world agreement.
   (c) Effect of the E.E.C.

Here then is the distilled essence of your speech, ideas created in your mind and shaped by reason. You should be able to describe them naturally in your own words, with a little practice. When the flow of words ceases, a glance at the next idea should restart the engine by switching your mind to a fresh train of thought.

Write your notes on a postcard, memorize them and look at them frequently. A good plan is to fix the card in a place that catches your eye at intervals during the day, so that you unconsciously photograph it, and could re-write the notes without difficulty at any moment. This will give you confidence, and you will gradually acquire the art of reading them mentally rather than visually, though it is always wise to have them in case you get a black-out.

A stiff card is better than a sheet of paper, as when nervous you will instinctively press a card and your nervousness will be unnoticed, whereas fluttering notes betray one every time! A card is also easier to handle, it can be laid down and picked up easily, put in your pocket, or behind your back, and it is graceful for gestures.

One card should be sufficient for a speech of ten to fifteen minutes, but a speech of half an hour or more would require a separate card for each main heading with further details. In the case of the Speech on Agriculture: —

Card 1 would be your complete outline – *i.e.* headings 1, 2, and 3, each with sub-headings A, B, and C.

Card 2 would be as follows: —

CARD 2.   POINT 1. – INDIVIDUAL FARMS.

(a) *Crops and Fertilizers.*
 Mixed or specialized farming.
 Fertilizers – Grants and research.

(b) *Labour and Wages.*
 Local – Imported – Harvest schemes.
 Wages compared to industry.

(c) *Marketing and Prices.*
 Guaranteed markets and prices.
 Producer to consumer.
 Development of canning and deep-freezing.

Card 3 would be developed in the same way *i.e.*

CARD 3.   POINT 2. – NATIONAL PLAN.

    (*a*) *State – Control or guidance?*
        Nationalization schemes.
        Freedom the price of security?
        State. Servant not master of free people.

    (*b*) *Rural Industries.*
        Interdependence of town and country.
        Engineering – electrical – Refrigeration and
        allied industries.
        Employment. Capital value – National
        balance.

    (*c*) *Rural Amenities.*
        Housing – schools – transport.
        Water – electricity – drainage
        Village halls – sports centres – playing fields.

Now try card 4 for yourself – head it

POINT 3. – WORLD ASPECT OF AGRICULTURE

and take each of the three sub-headings and divide them
into three further sub-headings. This method can be
developed indefinitely like the sets of boxes made in the
East, which fit into each other, and becomes smaller and
smaller until you have to pick out the last one with a
pin.

You will now realize the value of the original plan,
which was designed for a composite speech, or a series of
separate speeches, as each of these sections form the outline of interesting speeches, complete in themselves. This
concertina method of contracting and expanding, saves
hours of preparation, as the same outlines can be used
again and again, and fresh words, illustrations and up-to-
date facts, will spring naturally to the mind of a knowledgeable speaker – providing the *outline is his or her
own*. Success comes through the initial condensing of
matter, and mental concentration is essential, if reason
is to make a satisfactory job of producing clear outlines
from chaotic creative ideas.

Having done your four cards – fasten them together loosely in the corner opposite the number, otherwise when speaking you are very liable to place the card dealing with your finished section on top, instead of at the bottom of the stack as intended, and nothing is more disturbing than glancing at notes which do not refer to the matter in hand.

Green filing tags, used in most offices, are recommended for fastenings, as they take four cards comfortably and allow room for turning over easily. Train your mind to pause at the end of each section – glance over the appropriate card to see if you have left out any points then turn over and scan points of the new section before tackling it. Some speakers prepare sentences to act as links while doing this, but a deliberate pause shows mind control, and gives both speaker and audience welcome and necessary relaxation. High-pressure speeches are tiring and difficult to absorb.

Timing is a necessary habit of mind, and you should be able to judge how long it has taken you to develop any point, without constant reference to your watch. Many speakers have no idea of time and are a constant source of anxiety to a chairman, who has to work to a time table, or a secretary who has engaged the hall for a definite period, and has visions of the lights going out in the middle of a speech! A sense of time is equally important for a Chairman, and we all know the tale of the chairman who after speaking for thirty minutes instead of ten as he intended, called on the speaker for his address, only to be met with the reply: "My address Mr. Chairman is, 5 Chester Street, London, E.C.1A, 4QQ, and my train goes in ten minutes."

When practising speeches – time yourself strictly, allocating five minutes for each section of the speech divided as follows:

> Sub-headings (a) 2 minutes.
> Sub-headings (b) 1 minute.
> Sub-headings (c) 2 minutes.

The middle point is usually the least important and acts as a link between 1 and 3, but if it is the most important, alter your timing accordingly.

Strict timing is only necessary in speech training, as you do not want to be rigidly held to the clock when delivering your speech. That applies to all suggestions for training, which should be acted on conscientiously, but regarded as scaffolding, to be scrapped when feeling and reason can be safely left to construct and deliver a natural speech.

A rough guide to timing is to allow one-third of your time to the Approach and Conclusion, i.e. the Frame to your speech, which is dealt with in a later chapter, and two-thirds to the main section. This applies to speeches up to thirty minutes, for longer speeches, all the additional time should be devoted to development of points, as five minutes is the maximum required for Approaches or Conclusions.

Are you getting tired of notes, outlines, and reasoned designs? – well so am I, but lubrication is essential to the smooth running of your engine, and oil is a sticky substance. Oil your reasoning powers with good clear notes, and do not forget that the repetition of your main points, at the beginning, while developing, and at the end, will help you to focus your points, and the clear picture in your mind will interest you so much that you will forget to be nervous.

MEMORY

Let us now turn our attention to oil for the creative mind. The only help is a reminder of its own ideas, so memory, not notes, is the answer.

All normal people start with an adequate memory, as they start with all the attributes of a full and complete life, but some never develop it – some allow it to become rusty until they lose confidence in their own powers, and some improve it by constant use. Those who never develop it, are often the victims of faulty education on mass production lines. Would that teaching had always been less a matter of parrot-like repetition, and more on the lines of making children form, and express, their own constructive conclusions, based on what they have been taught. Not only does this stimulate creative thought, but in forming their conclusions, they store the facts more accurately and methodically for future use. Children should be taught to rely on themselves, and wise parents should send them shopping, from an early age, without a list, and send them back again for anything they have forgotten.

Memory is the mental filing system, which records impressions transmitted by the senses such as hearing, seeing, tasting, smelling, and touching, and your strongest faculty will record the deepest impression, which will therefore be the easiest to remember. Taste, smell, and touch do not help you to remember notes, so you have to rely on hearing and seeing, and as you get older – these faculties weaken, and it is advisable to reinforce them with the creative interest of association of ideas, *i.e.* linking up points into a chain of thought.

If your memory is to be trained on sound lines, most helpful to your individual mind, you must first examine the natural working of that mind, and test the varying recording strength of sight and sound and association of ideas. To discover your strongest faculty, try the following simple tests:

HEARING

Look in a shop window on the way to work in the morning, preferably one with which you are unfamiliar, and *repeat aloud* twelve articles displayed there. Turn your back to the window and repeat aloud a second time. If you cannot remember twelve without referring to the window, repeat exercise until you can name the twelve articles aloud without looking at them. Listen to yourself when repeating the list, and your ears should record a permanent impression, if your hearing is good.

On the way home in the evening, see how many articles you can remember, before reaching the shop, and then check yourself. If you can remember all twelve articles, then hearing is a strong faculty, in which case you should repeat your outlines for speeches *aloud*, listening intently to your own voice. With a little practice, you will probably be able to remember the outlines and the order of your points without much difficulty, though I should still advise you to have notes for reference. Notes recorded on a dictaphone and run off several times, often help this type of mind more than read outlines. If after several attempts you find you cannot remember more than eight out of twelve of the articles on the list, then test your sight.

Sight.

Do the same exercise, choosing a different shop, but this time, *write down* twelve articles, read the list once and do not refer to it again until you have tested your memory at the end of the day. If the result is more satisfactory than the test of hearing, then rely on your sight. Write your notes several times, memorize them, and put your card with main outline of speech in some prominent place, where it will catch your eye at intervals, and look at it last thing at night and first thing in the morning. By the time you come to deliver the speech, the photographic impression of your notes should be recorded so deeply in your mind, that you can read them mentally as well as visually, and if you lost them you could rewrite them without difficulty.

ASSOCIATION OF IDEAS

Now test your mind to see if it is interested in connecting ideas.

Again choose an unfamiliar shop, look in the window, and absorb as much as you can without either writing down or repeating aloud, and when checking up in the evening, see whether you visualize the articles in position in the window, and repeat them in the order in which they are arranged, or whether you instinctively group similar articles together. If you have chosen a haberdashery window for instance, how do you recall articles displayed? Do you make your list, starting from left to right of the window, or right to left, recalling articles consecutively as placed? If so, you have a photographic mind and are picturing the window as a whole when trying to remember your list. This confirms the sight test, and constant glances at your notes is your best method of memorizing.

If, on the other hand, you think of similar articles, say sewing materials, then fancy articles, and finally beauty preparations, or whatever happens to be in the window, then your mind enjoys linking up ideas, and you require notes built up on association of ideas. For this type of mind, I suggest the story-telling method outlined in the notes on "The Uses of Electricity" as this will help you by sustaining your interest. The same method may help you to memorize numbers, for example, 1248 might suggest doubling up each time, or 3407 be readily memorized by repeating 3 and 4 make 7.

Minds of this type are unusually fertile and imaginative and when trained should be very reliable.

Most people find writing down or repeating points aloud produces the best results. I like a combination of all known recording methods for safety's sake, so usually create my outline – link up points by connection of ideas, write them on a card – repeat out loud and then stick the card in my mirror where I observe it twice a day, but this is the foolproof method, as my memory has failed me once or twice, and I like to make double and trebly sure.

Having tested your memory, you will now know the best method of recalling points and if you have an average memory you should be able to recall eight out of twelve articles without any difficulty. A little memory training will enable you, in a very short time, to recall all twelve articles and this will give you confidence in yourself, and allow you to trust your memory, which will respond gallantly.

Now a word of hope for those whose memory has become rusty for want of practice. There are many well-known methods of memory training, but if you have a normally good memory that is temporarily below par, and merely needs toning up, you can invent your daily exercise to suit your own taste, thus ensuring the interest and co-operation of your creative mind.

If you are interested in flowers, note the different varieties and their arrangement in all the gardens down a certain road, and recall them on the return journey, but do not cheat, recall them before you reach that particular garden, and not when standing in front of it!

If you prefer people to flowers – imagine you are a witness in a magistrate's court and have to describe all the people you saw in a particular restaurant, or if you travel a lot by train – note the position of prominent advertisements, or whether the refreshment room is on the up or the down line, and check yourself on the return journey.

Any of these exercises will improve your memory surprisingly soon, but some form of exercise should be tried every day over a period of a month, as an occasional effort is as useless in toning up the memory as physical exercises done at long intervals would be in strengthening body muscles which have become flabby.

Having satisfied yourself that your lubricating system is adequate, and that your notes and a good memory will help both reason and imagination, you have now ensured the smooth delivery of your speech so you can now begin to study the speech from the angle of the audience. Repercussions are often unexpected and a wise speaker will seriously consider the comfort of the listeners if he hopes to retain interest.

5

Building the Body of your Speech

You will now want to journey into the realms of thought, and you will need to take other minds with you, so you must build a body worthy of your engine.

As the body of a car needs a steel frame to give it shape, springs, padding, and windows, so you need the equivalent in your speech.

FRAME

A frame is required to hold your passengers together and ensure that they are still with you at the end of the journey. The frame that holds a speech together is the repetition of your main points, thus controlling your flights of fancy, and bringing you back again and again to your planned design, and the hard substance of your argument. Just as the outlining of points at the beginning of the main section of your speech gives you clear mind direction, so it helps your audience to grasp the picture as a whole, and prevents undue criticism of minor points. Listeners will anticipate the particular point in which they are interested, and will travel with you tolerantly through intermediate stages, even if only mildly interested or bored, because they are eagerly anticipating your development of certain promised ideas later. This ensures the sustained interest of all sections, and if you refer to the main points at intervals, to mark the progress of your speech, you will not risk disappointing anyone by leaving out the anticipated point, which can so easily happen if your creative mind is not linked to a plan.

If this seems too rigid a method and your mind rebels against curbing free ideas unduly, adapt it, or reject it as you please, but I advise you to give it a fair trial first, as it is a method based on wide experience, and the analysis of effective speeches. Too often a speaker will develop the last point, which is probably the best, so attractively, with glowing phrases, and good illustrations, that the audience goes away absorbed with this one point to the exclusion of previous ones, so that the final impression stored away in their minds is incomplete. Repeating all the points at the end, restores the complete picture, and ensures that listeners retain and carry away *all* the main arguments.

SPRINGS

Springs are supplied by the tactful approach to possibly hostile minds, and as living speech should be thought provoking, therefore controversial, springs are essential. If you know there is a strong case against you, deal with it first, tactfully, humorously, and sympathetically, then having cleared the ground, you are in a far better position to build up your own case. Never make the mistake of putting your case first, and then dealing with the other side, as the final impression should be an overwhelming sense of irrefutability. Questions may weaken this impression, but many will be left unasked, if you can reply patiently that you have already given the answer, this makes the questioner look and feel foolish, and discourages others.

A good speaker examines the case from the opposing viewpoint, as in removing or discrediting objections, you are laying a sound foundation for your own case.

Another type of spring which eases travel is the link sentence, suggested in the last chapter for smooth transition from one point to the next. Nervous speakers may like to write out and memorize sentences which can be repeated mechanically during the switch over of their minds, but an experienced speaker will only need an idea connecting separate points, and if the order of your speech is logical, this should present no difficulty.

Minor springs which lessen the mental tension of audiences are vivid phrases, wise choice of words, the light touch in handling difficult points, and various suggestions, which may help you, will be found in the next chapter. Draw ease and comfort then from the springs 'of tact, humour, sympathy, and tolerance, and so simplify the journey for yourself and your passengers.

PADDING

Padding is the diluting of your food for thought to the capacity of your audience, and the presentation of such food in a colourful and easily digested form, which will bring the same ease to mind and body as good upholstery in a car. This can be achieved through the clarifying of ideas by means of illustrations, an adequate vocabulary of simple but illuminating words, and the use of metaphor and word pictures. The latter are particularly useful in the case of statistics, as the average mind cannot absorb figures and quickly loses interest. Use approximate, or the nearest round figures, *i.e.* the figure 249,950 would be better described as roughly a quarter of a million, and follow up with a word picture (such as the mile of pence used by the Red Cross in describing a target).

If the Press is present, it is best to read out the exact figure, then give the nearest round figure, then paint your picture. Supposing you were helping a national campaign to Save Bread, you might quote the exact figure of sacks of flour saved by one crust per day, and then work out the distance between two well-known towns which would be covered by sacks of flour laid end to end. Listeners will remember the journey marked by sacks more readily than the tons of flour.

WINDOWS

Windows for vision must be the wise use of your imagination, and some are more gifted in this respect than others, but it is a faculty you can encourage, and it will grow with the development of your personality. I once heard a clergyman say: "Imagination is the periscope through which we look over the dull, grey, walls of life", and I think that sentence sums up the power and depth of imagination, so there need be no shortage of glass for your windows.

Steel frame, springs, padding, and windows are all essentials, and reason will delight in using such material on building the perfect body for your speech. Your creative mind, however, will insist, rightly that the most comfortable body is useless, if the passengers are irritable, sleepy, quarrelsome, or discontented, and that you must put your passengers in the right frame of mind before beginning your journey. This brings us to the important question of Approaches and Conclusions, which should be prepared after the main section is complete, as you cannot decide how to handle your passengers until you know who you are likely to have and where you propose to take them.

Approaches and Conclusions

The Approach and Conclusion or Peroration of your speech, is the psychological side dealing with the attitude of mind of your audience. You must see that they are warm, relaxed and happy, as this current of friendliness is the invisible ray that opens the door to reason, and a stone cold audience will be irritated, rather than interested, by dry facts. If you are speaking on your own subject to those knowledgeable and keen, the right atmosphere exists already, and your task is easy, which explains why people can usually talk adequately on their own subject to those with similar interests.

Nothing is easy, however, in the thorough Right Way Method, which is designed to equip you for all types of meetings, and to speak on any subject with ease and confidence, so let us consider the approach to the average audience at a public meeting. You have before you people drawn from all walks of life, with varying degrees of interest in you or your subject. Many people go to meetings for all kinds of reasons unrelated to the matter in hand. They may have been brought by a friend, very reluctantly, the chairman may be their landlord, or an important person they dare not offend, a free meeting may attract passers-by out of the rain, and in the case of a political meeting, there may be the hope of a row, or, if it is not election time, the bribe in the form of a free tea or a conjuror.

Somehow or other you have to find a common denominator if you are to tune in to everybody from the start, and this can only be found in the realm of feelings which are common to all humanity. Just as the start of living speech is feeling, so the self-starter of constructive listening is also feeling, in fact the mental engine of your listeners works in exactly the same way as your own, namely through feeling to reason, so let us consider the various emotions most appropriate for your task, and most easily aroused.

At the start, the uppermost feeling in the mind of the average listener will be personal curiosity about the speaker, conjecture as to his or her ability to deal adequately with the subject, a certain veiled hostility if the subject is controversial, or if the subject is new, fear of the unknown will release the critical faculties. Curiosity, doubt, hostility, or criticism may be present, but there will be an underlying spirit of natural friendliness, coupled with British sportsmanship which is prepared to give you a chance, so your first job is to create a feeling of confidence in yourself, and all the potential irritants will dissolve.

A personal start is therefore a universal favourite and seldom fails, but it depends for success on perfect nerve control as the speaker must be relaxed, and able to talk naturally in conversational tones. This is not easy if your hands are trembling, your mouth dry, and your knees knocking together! Build your opening remarks round one idea, such as a reason for your interest in the subject, a personal experience or opinion, or an apt quotation, and talk confidentially, as if you were sharing a secret. You will find that the personal note commands attention through instinctive courtesy, but you need no notes, and no prepared phrases, just a warm friendly glance, without glasses if possible, a smile and a few simple words. If you are good at establishing friendly relations quickly, you will find it valuable, not only as a start, but also for recapturing attention which has wandered during your speech. Do not, however, give personal opinions when amplifying facts, as they should speak for themselves. Never make any Approach too long, remember the advice given in the first chapter: "If you do not strike oil in three minutes, stop boring!"

A good personal approach is obviously the best method of establishing confidence, but again I warn you that it is difficult in the early stages of public speaking, as a speaker may find that nervousness prevents the natural co-ordination of the creative, reasoned, and mechanical sections of the brain. This is often a temporary difficulty, but if you dread it, you are more likely to encounter it, and when you are unlucky, ideas will fail to penetrate your conscious mind. The only precaution against such a black-out is to prepare and memorize your opening phrases, so that your mechanical mind can fill the gap with a recitation, while you are regaining mind control. It is a poor alternative to a natural opening, and I hope only a temporary one, but better than a breakdown, which, far from gaining the confidence of your audience, would shatter your own.

Faults to avoid in a personal approach are apologies, which depreciate your stock unnecessarily, and undue modesty, which does not ring true, as, if you do not know enough about the subject you should never have considered speaking on it, and above all, never contradict any flattering introduction made by your Chairman, as the implication is that he is either a fool or a liar!

Having introduced yourself, it is quite a good idea to introduce the audience to each other, in some phrase such as: "We have here to-day visitors from overseas, students still at university, mothers taking a well-earned rest from domestic duties, and young men and women on the threshold of their careers, all gathered together to consider a vital problem touching us all". Each section to which you refer will take it as a personal message of welcome, and it will create a community spirit, in which friendliness will develop naturally.

Confidence, then, is the first thing to establish, and though you may gain it later by the skilful development of your argument, a poor start will increase your nervousness and make your task more difficult, so practise friendly openings in conversation, and later you can apply them to speeches.

The next important point is to satisfy the curiosity of your listeners as to the subject of your speech, which you hope to do by outlining your main headings, but you can do so sooner by making the focal point the subject of your opening remarks. If you deal with it in an original and arresting way, and make it the recurring theme all through your speech, it can be very effective.

This method was illustrated at a meeting into which I wandered by chance, because it was raining and I wanted to think out a speech of my own! I never heard the Chairman, but suddenly a vigorous voice cut across my thoughts in these words:

"As the Chairman has told you, I want to speak on Bureaucracy. I have just returned from the East, and the most vivid impression left on my mind was of seeing a swarm of locusts stripping a tree. Now I am convinced that if you let a swarm of bureaucrats and civil servants loose on the tree of industry, the effect will be exactly the same!!" Possibly a superficial view, but nevertheless a colourful start, and as the subject of his talk was the sixteen Government departments to which he had been referred in negotiating a business deal, he carried the idea through by pausing, as if at the entrance to each new Government department and saying with a wave of his hand: "Look, *another* swarm of locusts".

This opening arrested attention by the personal experience and the focal point (*i.e.* the disastrous effects of bureaucracy) became the theme note, which the speaker struck well and truly all through the speech.

An opening of this kind would satisfy your creative mind as it would establish confidence, and allay curiosity, and make your hearers willing and eager to follow you, but it depends for success on imagination and you alone can give birth to it, as it is a reflection of your personality, that powerful 10 per cent leaven already mentioned.

For speakers whose minds are more factual than imaginative, a personal opening is difficult, and in any case all speakers need to ring the changes, so when training your mind in approach methods, take the main outline of a speech in which you are interested, and try each of the following approaches:—

DIFFERENT TYPES OF APPROACHES.	FEELINGS AROUSED.
1. Personal note.	Friendliness.
2. Introduction of audience.	Friendliness.
3. Focal point as theme note.	Sustained interest.
4. Topical note.	Quick interest.
5. Word spelling.	Mutual interest.

DIFFERENT TYPES OF APPROACHES.	FEELINGS AROUSED.
6. Local colour.	Sympathy.
7. Historical background.	Memory.
8. Humour.	Humour.
9. Controversy.	Anger.
10. Startling opening.	Surprise.

The Topical Note is self-explanatory, matters of general interest in the daily press, an announcement on the wireless, reference to important visitors connected with the subject of the speech, anything which is already in the minds of the majority, will strike a responsive chord at the outset, but the reference must be of current interest, and up-to-date, what the Press calls "hot" news.

Word Spelling may be a novel approach to some and is worth trying, especially by those who have difficulty in remembering the order of their points. Take a short appropriate word, and make each of your points begin with one of the letters, so that the complete set of points spell the word. If your subject was "The Importance of Agriculture to the Town Dweller" you might take the word EAT for example and make your three points: —

1. Employment.
2. Assurance.
3. Trade.

The main thing is to explain the method to the audience by telling them in this case that you are going to talk about the word EAT, because the three main benefits we gain from agriculture apart from food, begin with the three letters. Spelling the word, namely E for Employment, A for Assurance, and T for Trade. As you come to each point, reiterate the word, and make your conclusion fit your approach by suggesting that every time we EAT, we should remember the farmer with gratitude. This method is only suitable for simple audiences, educational talks, or talks to children, but it invites, and usually receives, the co-operation of the audience. It is better to choose your word after you have shaped the outline in your mind and selected the main headings. The latter can often be changed to similar words beginning with the right letter, for instance the second point in EAT may have been Insurance against starvation, which could be altered to Assurance.

Local Colour is useful when travelling round the country, as districts and counties are apt to be insular, and imagine that a visiting lecturer is disinterested in their local difficulties. Local knowledge gleaned beforehand as an opening will dispel this impression, but only use it as a brief approach, and do not waste much time on local matters about which the audience is already familiar. Sympathy over unemployment, congratulations on new industries likely to provide work, an invitation to the audience to supply local knowledge for you to take back with you are all examples of local colour likely to establish a sympathetic bond with your listeners. Local knowledge is always a good start with high officials visiting branches of an organization.

Historical background is a thought-provoking approach, particularly useful for a dull subject, where you want to stir up general interest as a forerunner to an appeal for recruits or funds. Details of the birth and growth of an organization will often give a more inspiring picture of its importance and future possibilities, than details of the present organization, as you are describing a living organism rather than dealing with dry facts. Care must be taken to time an historical approach, as, if you are interested in history, you may be tempted to make the approach two-thirds of the speech!

Humour. I hesitate to recommend humour as it can prove disastrous, but obviously laughter dissolves barriers very effectively, so test yourself as a humorist, and if you know a suitable story relevant to your subject, and can tell it briefly and well, and do not forget the point, then by all means begin with humour.

At a Speakers' Competition for farmers at which I was the judge, the subject was "Town Ignorance on Country Matters", and the winner got away to a splendid start with the following: A townsman called Jim rang up his brother, living in the country, and asked, "How goes it, George?" George replied that he was terribly busy, in the midst of lambing, Jim asked again, "How goes it?" and on receiving the answer that the weather was making matters very difficult, suggested, "Why not postpone the lambing until the weather improves!"! This type of story combines humour with the focal point of the speech, and rightly gained high marks for the speaker, as it was much appreciated by a country audience, and their laughter at once put him at his ease.

Controversy is dangerous before you have developed your theme, but carrying the war into the enemy's camp is sometimes necessary in a debate, if you cannot tempt him to come out, but this method is unwise in a speech, as it arouses fierce emotion, which may tend to submerge reason, whereas reason must be convinced if the gist of a speech is to be remembered.

A Startling Opening is as stimulating as a startling event, but we are all so jaded these days, by day-to-day events of great importance, that few statements are capable of galvanizing an audience into life.

Here then, are different types of approaches on which to practise, try them out on a dictaphone or better still at a meeting, and analyse the results until you feel confident to handle any type of audience. Such confidence will be your greatest asset, and the only way to acquire it is practice in framing facts, so begin with the two speeches on Coal and Chairs which you have already developed. The following suggestions for approaches may help you:—

APPROACHES FOR PREVIOUS SPEECH ON COAL

1. *Personal.*
    (*a*) Random thoughts on coal arising from fireside meditation.
    (*b*) Description of personal visit to coal mine.
    (*c*) Account of recent meeting on importance of coal which aroused your interest in a new subject.

2. *Topical.*
You have all read in the papers recently about the rise and fall in coal production and our attention turns naturally to coal in its relation to prosperity throughout the world.

3. *Word Spelling.*
As the Chairman has told you Coal is our subject and

I propose to consider four points, each presenting a question to our minds, and to help you to remember them I have made each point begin with a letter of the short word FUEL – they are: —

F. Fuel. Is coal the best?
U. Uses of coal. What of the future?
E. Employment. Is it shrinking or expanding?
L. Legislation. How far should the State control coal and its bye-products.
Fuel – Uses – Employment and Legislation.

F – U – E – L

4. *Local Colour.* (If meeting is held in neighbourhood of Mines).

Many of you in this area will be aware that the mining industry has contracted dramatically in the years since the war. We all know of mines around here which have closed down in the last few years, and how difficult it can be for miners to get other jobs. But looking to the future, we can now see an ever increasing need for coal to fuel the Nation's power stations, and we can predict a new need to recruit miners again. I propose to discuss a few random thoughts about this which might occur to any of us, then consider the life and working conditions of miners, and finally discuss the bigger question of the future of the coal industry.

5. *Historical Background.*

Looking back over history, we find that coal enabled Great Britain to become the leading industrial Nation in the 19th century, but that the cost was the destruction of much English countryside, and many famous beauty spots. Today, the coal industry is still one of the most important in the country, and the National Union of Mineworkers is one of the most influential. Therefore, we have to ask ourselves, has the development of the industry brought with it benefits to compensate for the cost? Let us consider this question from the point of view of the ordinary citizen, the miners and the Nation.

6. *Humour.*

A man travelling recently to the U.S.A. received a telegram from his lawyer on his arrival saying: "Regret to inform you that your mother-in-law has died. Shall we bury, cremate, or embalm her?" A prompt reply was despatched: "Bury, cremate, and embalm her, take no risks". Like that man, I suggest that we take no risks with Coal, which is essential to our comfort as individuals, and our prosperity as a nation. Everyone should study the facts of the fuel shortage, so that the collective wisdom of the nations should be mobilized behind any far-reaching decisions.

7. Startling or Unusual Opening.

This would naturally be the individual choice of the speaker as what is startling to some minds is commonplace to others, but we would all probably be startled if a prim and proper looking person, whom one expected to be dull, began with a swear word.

These seven examples are ordinary approaches, which might be used as simple conversational openings by any speaker with no special knowledge or eloquence, who is not attempting oratory, but merely anxious to create a friendly interest in himself and his subject. We will now take the same standard openings and apply them to the speech on Chairs (Chapter 2).

SUGGESTED APPROACHES FOR A SPEECH ON CHAIRS

1. Personal.

At university we all thought of Home with varying degrees of homesickness. The thing I missed most was my comfortable armchair, and every time I lit my pipe, I longed to sink back in my special pet, a Queen Anne chair, of great age, with a high back and side wings to keep out the draughts, a well-sprung seat, and cushions covered in attractive tapestry, which has suffered all manner of ill-usage and still looks inviting! This invariably started a train of thought about chairs, and I realized for the first time, what a fascinating subject it can be, and decided to study them, when time permitted such a luxury. Today I want to talk about chairs and their history, materials, and coverings, and then to consider period and symbolic chairs.

2. Topical.

This is an age of comfort and as chairs contribute more

to personal comfort than most furniture, with the possible exception of beds, we all have our own ideas about them, and I thought they might prove a fruitful subject for a short talk.

3. *Word Spelling.*
Let us take the letters of the word CHAIR and make them our guide to points for consideration in our talk this afternoon.

>C   Comfort.
>H   History.
>A   Art.
>I   Individuality.
>R   Reproduction.

4. *Local Colour.*
Here in the district where Chippendale lived, one cannot help regretting that the speeding up of this modern age has largely replaced the craftsmanship of such men with modern utility, so that their masterpieces are rare and valuable, possessed only by the fortunate few! If some of you still have genuine examples, I hope you will invite me to see them, meantime I would like to discuss with you the subject of chairs.

5. *Historical.*
Chairs are cameos of history through the ages, and tell us by their shape, coverings, and the material of which they are made, much of the habits, customs, costumes, and architecture of the different periods which contributed to their design.

6. *Humour.*
The acid test of a good speaker is his ability to make his audience forget their hard chairs, and I hope to arouse your interest in chairs to such an extent that you will forget the impression on your anatomy of your particular specimen! Let us consider five aspects of the subject, viz:

7. *Startling or Unusual Openings.*
If you saw "Danger – handle with care" on the back of chairs you might give them more consideration. As it is, the moment we think about them most vividly is probably when we view with horror the mangled wreck

of a valuable chair, the back of which has been broken, through our thoughtlessness in tipping it up, and putting our full weight on the back legs. Another moment which makes an impression, in more ways than one, is when we fall through a deck chair, because we have not set it up properly. Such thoughtlessness is responsible for the high casualty list among chairs, and possibly a little reflection on their value and uses' may save the lives of a few chairs in the future.

These examples of the same set of approaches used for different subjects should help you, especially as the subjects were as ordinary and uninspiring as Coal and Chairs, but only constant practice will enable you to tune in quickly to your audience. Do not aim at oratory, or colourful passages, leave those for the conclusion, as the start should be in simple language which you would use if conversing with a friend. For this reason, I have chosen everyday subjects and ordinary approaches, and I crave the indulgence of the experienced speaker, who will probably consider them too elementary, but beginners must learn to use natural language, and they can raise the standard of their oratory as their vocabulary and power of speech develop. To them I would say persevere with this exercise and you will be well repaid as nothing gives you greater confidence than happy relations with your audience. Take three points on each of a dozen subjects and try fitting them with different approaches. This will train your mind to recognize and select an appropriate one when desired, and will also save you much time and trouble later, as standard approaches with which you are familiar, can be used again and again, provided you paint them in fresh colours to sustain the interest of your creative mind.

A successful approach is a sure method of putting your audience in a good mood at the start, but it is equally important that you part happily, though reluctantly, at the end, so a word about conclusions.

This comes after you have summed up your points, and is a direct appeal to emotion, as powerful as possible. As with Approaches, no notes are required unless possibly a key word suggesting the main idea. Quotations are very popular, but they must be memorized and sound spontaneous or the force of your final appeal will be weakened, whereas it should rise in intensity, and carry your audience to the summit, leaving them filled with emotion.

A pause before an outburst of clapping is the supreme tribute to speakers, as it means that they have aroused such powerful emotions that the purely mechanical action of clapping has been temporarily suspended.

If your speech is devoted to practical ends, and you want your listeners to show their appreciation by certain definite action, end on a constructive note, after the surge of emotion has subsided, as the final impression is all-important. Remain standing until the applause has died down and then say quietly: "Ladies and gentlemen, I knew you would feel strongly on this matter and I am glad, but remember that feeling is only the start of action, so ask yourself, What can I do to express my feelings adequately? My suggestion is so and so, but your answer to the question will vary according to your individual circumstances, and I hope Madam Chairman that many valuable suggestions will be forthcoming at question time". Your chairman, if experienced, will repeat your suggestion in thanking you, and that will be the final emphasis to the audience which should produce results earned by your eloquence.

Conclusions should fit in with Approaches, strike the same note, *i.e.* if you begin with a quotation from Shakespeare refer to it at the end and cap it with another, or if you begin with a question, repeat it with the answer in the finish, and so you will get your facts embedded in feeling, just as the passengers in your car are happy and comfortable, both mentally and physically, while your engine carries them along swiftly and smoothly.

6

Colour and Polish

Development of Personality — Vivid Phrases and the Power of Words

If the last chapter has convinced you of the need for a colourful frame for your facts and has taught you how applied psychology can help you to construct such frames, it will have shown you how your thoughts, if naturally expressed, act as powerful magnets to attract the interest of other minds.

This surely is the secret of personality, which we are told is indefinable, sharing one's innermost thoughts with others, drawing out their thoughts in return, and re-vitalizing our minds with the fascinating interchange of ideas which must follow such a process. In this way we keep our minds fresh and colourful and natural speaking must develop personality because nature intended indi-vidual thoughts to emerge through the power of speech, thus expressing the personality of the speaker. The ghastly proportion of colourless personalities in the world, is due to the curb placed by man-made restrictions on the natural expression of natural thought. Reason has been exalted by a scientific age until it has become a barrier between feeling and voice instead of fulfilling its natural function of a controlling force, directing ideas to practical ends, curbing and releasing power as required.

When Nature created mankind she never contemplated a T.V. set in every home, an all-powerful daily press which can make or break a speaker and must therefore be placated, a law of libel which tells us that the greater the truth the greater libel, a Parliament where questions can be asked in the searchlight of criticism and a nation of people taught to accept rather than create ideas. These things have killed great oratory, as people no longer feel, think, and speak naturally, they prefer to express the popular feelings of the day and keep their real feelings to themselves, thus erecting a barrier in place of Nature's window through which she meant the human soul to shine out through the medium of voice, eyes, and gestures.

In place of that window this mechanized age has erected dummy windows reflecting artificial light, and heat provided by others, small wonder personality is the exception rather than the rule. If a determined effort is not made to break down this artificial barrier we are in danger of becoming a nation of ostriches, avoiding the facing of unpleasant facts, and relying on soft words as feathers to keep out any sensations of cold or heat, or any other unpleasant feelings which might disturb. No speaker should ever debase the currency of speech to animal level, it is shirking responsibility to refuse to observe and think on facts, and the feathers in this case are the white feathers of moral cowardice, grown to protect you from the icy blasts of criticism, disapproval, and opposition, or from the heat generated by an enthusiastic mind which stirs your conscience and makes you uncomfortable.

Nature however will not be denied, and the mere conscious rejection of emotion and the subsequent development of a colourless personality is not the end of the story. Tragedy follows, as the creative mind still functions and produces thoughts and feelings which lead to frustration and inhibitions if unreleased by speech, and the injury which you do to your self-respect by moral cowardice in refusing to express your thoughts, freely and honestly, will create self-contempt, which is far more hurtful than the contempt of others. An imprisoned mind knows all the horrors of a concentration camp, and much harm has been done to the delicate mechanism of natural speech, by a conventional age with its artificial code of manners and habits, and its wicked belief that children should be seen and not heard. Why should public opinion, moulded by a handful of so-called experts, be accepted unquestionably as standards of thought on which to base speeches. After all even George Robey in his wisdom used to tell us, with that inimitable arch of eyebrow, "We may all be cast in the same mould but some are definitely mouldier than others!"

Here then is the cause of colourless personality and one of the main reasons for writing this book is to convince would-be speakers that the first essential to success is the release of sincere emotion in natural and honest language. Readers who have carried out the suggested exercises conscientiously will have pierced the artificial windows many times and will now reap their reward, for the natural sunlight of their own personality can shine through their speeches and illuminate them, and they can discard the artificial heat and light which colour so many unconvincing and unreal speeches. The more you observe and think on current events, the more you will encourage your creative mind to conceive original ideas as a result of applying your feeling and imagination to facts and training will have taught you how to express such ideas. You will also have learned that reason is necessary for such expression, not to stifle ideas, but to control in the interests of kindliness, tolerance, discretion, accuracy, and knowledge. Without this control you are in danger of unleashing a powerful emotional force with catastrophic results, like the driver of a car without brakes who has no idea of the strength of his engine. Speakers who have never realized the importance of harnessing reason to emotion and who are driven solely by burning conviction have swayed multitudes for good or evil, but such power if uncontrolled can do immense harm, as it reflects a one-track mind and usually ends in fanaticism.

On the other hand, speeches based on cold reasoning and scientific fact can be equally harmful, as they ignore emotions, and dry up the natural springs of human relationship by killing faith and destroying character. I had a personal experience of a girl driven to suicide after an unfortunate love affair by the speech of an eminent scientist who convinced her that there was no survival after death. By killing her faith he removed the fear of the consequences of suicide and deprived her of the hope that the tangle would be straightened out in another world. Such power is dangerous and the Right

Way method seeks to construct original ideas, propel them by the force of sincere feeling and use reason to control that feeling and supply the knowledge – the architecture, and the skilful handling of the mechanics of voice, health, and nerve control.

Mechanics of speech is the third and final stage of training and is the subject for Chapters 8 and 9 on "Nervousness" and "Delivery", but before leaving the all-important subject of personality, I would like to give you a few hints which may help your self-expression, under the headings of vivid phrases, metaphors, analogies, and the choice of words.

Vivid Phrases

These must spring naturally from your own mind as they are the reflection of your personality but they need not be original and are often based on glowing words by which you were attracted at some time or other in conversation, speeches, or articles. Your mind unconsciously stored them for future use and suggests them to you at a later date when the gist of the speech or article is forgotten. Many which you could use with advantage are forgotten, so give your imagination a good paint box by collecting colourful phrases that appeal to you, and writing them down at the time.

Churchill was a past master of the glowing word and even when he had to speak a prepared brief, he would pause at intervals and sum up his own conclusions at that point in some inimitable and unforgettable phrase. I well remember his speech on the future Peace Conference when he finished by imploring us "not to let the eagles be brought down by the squawking parrots". How prophetic and how illuminating because it focused attention on the outstanding point of his speech in one vivid phrase. Again none of us will ever forget the meaning, even when we cannot recall the exact words, of phrases coined by him which will go down to history such as his promise of Blood, Toil, Tears, and Sweat, or his clarion call to the Nation when he warned Germany that we would fight on the beaches, fight in the trenches, fight in the villages, and fight in the streets. I have purposely refrained from giving an exact quotation because if your mind suggests a quotation which you had not intended to use, and cannot remember accurately, you should use it nevertheless as it is obviously the right colouring for your point and if you reject it you will set up a feeling of frustration in your creative mind which will impede your work. Safeguard yourself by some such phrase as: "I cannot remember the exact words, perhaps somebody in the audience can tell us afterwards, but it ran something like this . . ."

Do not be content with stock quotations – make your own selections. The following are less known Churchillian phrases which attracted me and you can add many from your own store.

"By singleness of purpose, by steadfastness of conduct, by tenacity and endurance such as we have so far displayed – by these, and only by these, can we discharge our duty to the future of the world and to the destiny of man."

"The day will come when the joybells will ring again throughout Europe, and when victorious nations will plan and build in justice, in tradition, and in freedom, a house of many mansions."

"The destiny of mankind is not decided by material computation. When great causes are on the move in the world, stirring all men's souls, drawing them from their firesides, casting aside comfort, wealth, and the pursuit of happiness in response to impulses at once awestriking and irresistible, we learn that we are spirits, not animals, and that something is going on in space and time, and beyond space and time, which, whether we like it or not, spells duty."

"When the King declares war, the Empire is at war. The darkest moment came. Did anyone flinch? Was there one cry of pain or doubt or terror? No, Sir, darkness was turned into light and into a light which will never fade away."

These quotations are from the Calendar of Wit and Wisdom called *Grim and Gay,* and have been chosen because they all deal with fundamental issues and are calls to deep emotional impulses which after all are the final arbiters of history. A study of famous oratory enlarges one's vocabulary, and increases appreciation of the beautiful English language, and the Appendix to this book dealing with speeches which have made history, may prove helpful, but speeches that appeal to me may be useless to you, as your mind should be selective; so start a collection of your own.

Vivid phrases are even more valuable than quotations and once you acquire the habit of collecting them you will find material in your everyday work, while conversations with strangers often prove a fruitful field. An American told me that a popular slogan in New York during the black market activities was: "Over the ceiling, under the counter, and behind the door". It made me laugh so I jotted it down, also the words of another speaker who, in countering the opinion that greed was the cause of black markets, suggested that need was equally responsible and finished his remarks by saying: "Money may be the root of all evil but the want of it is the whole blooming tree!"

Daily papers and magazines often supply vivid phrases.

Consistent picking out of apt sentences will interest your mind and start it coining its own phrases, which will be more vivid and more effective, as they will bear the imprint of your own mind, and in the next chapter I will deal with a filing system for storing such colouring matter, in addition to whatever method you may have adopted for dealing with speech material.

Metaphors and Analogies
The use of metaphor denotes well-focused points, as it is only when your mind has a clear picture of an idea that it will observe similarities, *i.e.* Nature's use of sun and rain would be a suitable analogy when picturing character developed through happiness and sorrow, similarly, night following day could illustrate cause and effect, and familiar proverbs are easy methods used by lazy speakers to illustrate obvious truths.

One illustration should be sufficient, but if you must use more than one, be careful not to mix your metaphors even if they are equally applicable to the point. We all know the speaker who tells us not to swop horses in midstream, not to fiddle while Rome is burning, not to take our eyes off the ball, and not to talk to the man at the wheel. In the end we do not know whether we are riding a horse, practising our violin, playing golf, or motoring, and our minds are dizzy from such sudden switches, whereas the point is probably that we must concentrate and avoid distractions, just the very thing which the speaker is unable to do himself.

When illustrating a point always make the point first, then give the illustration, and then repeat the point, so as to bring your mind back to your argument. Analogies are as invaluable for driving home points as they are for approaches and conclusions because they focus attention on points, and act in the same way as spotlights in a theatre.

Clear, purposeful thinking should crystallize ideas into appropriate speech and suggest suitable metaphors, colourful phrases, and the correct use of words, and suitable gestures and voice should follow, as you will automatically set in motion the whole intricate speech mechanism as explained in Chapter 9 on "Delivery", but before leaving the creative side of speaking, I would suggest that you ponder on the immense power of creative speech, and realize the repercussion of your ideas on other minds.

You will often find that harm may be done to a good cause by an attack on some minor defect. I well remember hearing a slashing attack on the Church by an ardent supporter who was angered by the behaviour of one clergyman. The impression on my mind was that the Church was a dangerous institution and most clergy were of this type, whereas had the speaker begun by saying that because Church influence was vitally necessary in world affairs he did not wish it to be discredited by the action of *one* misguided clergyman, he could still have delivered his attack, but the impression conveyed to his listeners would have been very different.

Alternatively, analysis often proves that so-called attacks on a system are really attacks on the abuses of that system, and debaters can often dumbfound their opponents by agreeing that all these abuses can, and should, be remedied, which would make the system they are defending even more perfect than at present.

Choice of Words.

Just as a wise choice of metaphors follows the clear focusing of points, so appropriate words should suggest themselves if you are intent on painting a word picture, and thus prevent over or under-emphasis. If, for example, you are thinking of the effect of an atomic bomb you would naturally use a word like "catastrophic" or "appalling", as they are pregnant with meaning, whereas "nasty" or "unpleasant" would seem singularly inappropriate. On the other hand, the intense speaker who puts a heart-throb into each word and describes everyday events as "miraculous" or "stupendous", and remarks that the weather is "just too, too terrible" is equally lacking in a sense of proportion. If you listen to the description of something seen through a telescope, you will be struck by the brevity of the sentences used by the speaker. Because he has complete concentration, he automatically uses the minimum number of words to convey an intelligible and interesting picture, and his mind suggests no unnecessary padding. That is the secret of good speech, simple, direct language with words used sparingly, adjectives chosen wisely, and the sincerity of the unfettered mind behind the tongue lighting up the picture, so that the ideas are transferred alive with the certainty that they will germinate and grow in other minds.

As a general rule avoid popular slang as it imparts a stale flavour to your speech and takes the sparkle out of it, though an occasional colloquialism may be permitted and is often effective. If used, see that it is up to date, *i.e.* "wizard" and "shooting a line" were appropriate during the war when they were the current coin of speech in the Air Force just as "too, too divine" was a popular, though inane saying amongst the bright young things of the early thirties, but all these words would sound meaningless today, as words, like ladies' fashions, change with the times. Florid and ornate styles are as much out of date today as the useless bric-a-brac that cluttered up Victorian drawing-rooms, and the best effects are achieved by simple architecture, clear meanings, the subdued colouring of reflective thought, and the polish of natural culture.

Just as the furnishings of a house reflect personality so the choice of words stamps a speaker's individuality on his speech. Vivid phrases, metaphors, quotations and stories, if the latter are suitable for the platform, which alas so many are not, provide the colour and polish for speeches, but the colours will be dim and the polish dull if the apt word does not present itself spontaneously. This requires an adequate vocabulary.

Words must remain the servant of inspiring ideas but when I mentioned at the start of this book that speaking is more a matter of perspiration than inspiration, I might have added that control of inspiration causes perspiration. A large measure of this control consists in pruning words and learning to handle them skilfully, so Chapters 10 and 11 are devoted to Words and Phraseology.

Before closing this chapter on Colouring, I would remind you that all speech colouring must be individual and colourful words, phrases or thoughts are usually fleeting and illusive, often flashing into the mind at inappropriate moments only to be lost if not captured at once for use in the future, which requires some sort of mental file.

7

Filing Systems

Just as a well-run office has a good filing system so that all information is at hand when required, so your reasoning faculties will demand a good reference library and some effective way of storing facts. This is comparatively easy and all speakers should collect data and store it methodically, or should know where to go in search of information. What is more difficult, and even more important, is a filing system for the colouring matter mentioned in the previous chapter, which you will use naturally and with great effect while speaking, if it is readily accessible. The following suggestions may help you to record both Facts and Impressions.

Recording facts. If you have not already got one, choose any good filing system suitable for your purpose, and keep your facts revised and add to them frequently. Keep abreast of current publications, cultivate a catholic taste to broaden your mind, and when you get a mass of detailed information on any subject, predigest it by picking out all the important points and making a precis of them for future use. The best way to condense articles is to read them several times, form your own conclusions, then sum up in a concise sentence which you can introduce into a speech. This prevents breaking the contact with your audience by reading extracts from the article. If you say: "I read an interesting article by —— the gist of which was —— the effect is far better, and more spontaneous, than quotations, and if you have the article with you for reference, you can always quote extracts in answer to questions, or hand the article round after the meeting. If using this method, it is advisable to write out your summary in a notebook kept for the purpose, adding the reference number of the article and the title of a possible speech to which it might relate. Writers sometimes do this for you, for example, a war correspondent summing up General Montgomery's strategy at the Battle of Ardenne used these words: "Montgomery's strategy was to Head Off, Seal Off, and Write Off – and as this summed up the article admirably my entry in a notebook marked Articles and their Conclusions was as follows: —

Subject.	Source.	Ref. No.	Summing Up.
War strategy	Correspondent describing Montgomery's strategy (Name & date of paper)		Head off Seal off Write off

This method can be used for recording impressions of books to which you wish to refer, either chapter by chapter, or a final summary, and can also be used for filing colouring matter as you will see later in this chapter.

Keep a card index of your speeches and file your typed notes, which should be on cards strung together and numbered. These skeleton speeches can be used repeatedly providing that the bones are covered each time with the living flesh of new facts, and dressed in fresh colourful ideas and illustrations, but if the skeleton itself is not your own child, you will have great difficulty in breathing life into it and will rarely succeed.

Experience will teach you the most helpful method of recording facts, and outside help is always available so this is not an unsurmountable difficulty. The chief problem will be finding time to devote to this necessary corollary of good speech making, but it will repay to overhaul your store of knowledge at regular intervals. Never be content with old notes (except skeletons) or obsolete facts, as stale matter produces stale speeches and bored audiences.

Recording Ideas.
Now let us turn to the filing system required by your creative mind for storing colouring matter, *i.e.* sparks that lit your imagination, or gems of thought that occurred to you at singularly inappropriate moments,

often in your bath or in the middle of the night. Unless you consciously capture and record them they will gradually fade and will not spring to your mind when required to illuminate some important point, which would be a pity as they are the means of impressing your personality on your speeches.

The mechanical action of writing down impressions records them more permanently, and though all speakers must evolve a filing system suitable to their mentality, the following method which I have used successfully for many years may be worth a trial. You have already been advised to collect vivid phrases, metaphors and analogies, quotations, and stories so let us limit our filing system to such material and you can adapt it to any other material as you think fit.

Most minds, observe selectively, *i.e.* matters in which they were previously interested, but if you train your powers of observation to be more general, you will collect a rich store of colouring matter which your creative mind will delight to use as an antidote for drab dreary facts. Study Nature, always a fruitful field from which many effective analogies can be drawn, as reference to animal habits appeal to audiences. Any evolutionary process has a parallel in the growth of trees or flowers, and gardens are always popular.

To record these ideas for future use is a gradual process as your mind likes time to bring the cream to the surface and reject the mediocre, so skim your collection daily, weekly, and quarterly, and make the latter your permanent store.

1. *Daily Collection.*

Tear out or mark any interesting points which remain in your mind after skimming the daily paper or reading current publications. Devote quarter of an hour, in the evening if possible, to recalling the day's impressions. Write down any striking remarks heard in speeches, or conversations, as only vivid phrases with special appeal to your mind will be retained after the lapse of some hours, and such phrases will come to the surface with telling effect at some future time if consciously recorded. Popular papers are best for colouring matter, as they are usually superficial, and strive for effect rather than education, whereas serious reading demands time and concentration. Put your daily collection into a drawer and forget about it.

2. *Weekly Revision*.

At the end of the week run over your varied assortment and discard all that seems futile on second thoughts, which is usually about 50 per cent. Divide what is left into large envelopes, suitably marked, *i.e.* Colourful phrases, Quotations, Metaphors, Stories or Articles. Leave this selected colouring to simmer in your mind ready for the third and last skimming.

3. *Quarterly Revision*.

After two refreshers your mind will have thoroughly absorbed this colouring matter, and you can now go through each envelope systematically, and transfer what still seems worth while into notebooks, marked to correspond with your envelopes. My notebooks are tabulated on the lines suggested for precis of articles, illustrations are linked with ideas, quotations with subjects, and analogies with points which they might illustrate aptly. This triple revision of colouring matter sets up a permanent record in your subconscious mind, and enables you to find the appropriate illustration, when your reasoned mind has focused a point which it wants to emphasize. Colourful illustrations should emerge spontaneously from your mental store, as does the artist's choice of paint when colouring his picture, and the wider your range of colours the more vivid your speech will be, and the more it will reflect your personality.

Good speaking has four essentials, marshalling of facts, persuasive appeal, colouring matter, and proper use of your voice. We have dealt with the first three fairly exhaustively in the workshops of Reason and Imagination, so now turn to the mechanics of the voice. Good delivery should automatically follow correct mind direction, but nervousness must first be overcome, or it will intervene between ideas and voice.

8

Nervousness

Nervousness is nervous energy, that mysterious force generated and propelled by feeling, which affects your whole nervous system, either shattering it or alternatively, gearing it up until you are tense and vibrant and capable of reaching heights of oratory.

If this energy is misdirected by Fear it can throw your whole nervous system out of gear with the most disastrous results, and it is fear of this misdirection which makes us regard nervous energy as a potential enemy, forgetting that it is a vital factor in all creative art, as it makes us sensitive and receptive, and without it we should be dead and devoid of feeling. Could we eliminate it we would be crazy to do so, as we would be quenching the vital spark. The would-be speaker who congratulates himself or herself on not being nervous is merely ignorant of the workings of the mind, and will never achieve much, as his limit will be brain and voice without the dynamic force of feeling.

On the other hand, nervous energy, correctly controlled by knowledge, sincerity, honesty, enthusiasm, or any of the constructive emotions can produce the best that is in us. How then can we ensure perfect nerve control? The only way is to remove the cause of misdirection and see that the controlling emotion is the right one, just as a driver must learn to handle his gears skilfully before he is safe on the road. Gradually he gains the necessary self confidence when he finds his hands automatically making the right movements and nervousness vanishes, with fear of misdirection. So it is with speaking, banish Fear and with it will go Nervousness, so let us consider Fear and its causes.

As far as speakers are concerned there are six main reasons for Fear.

1. Fear of the unknown.
2. Fear of being misunderstood.
3. Fear of the audience.
4. Fear of inaudibility.
5. Fear of oneself.
6. Fear of the physical reaction of speaking.

The Right Way method of speech training is based on the elimination of these six Fears, and if you have mastered each chapter and done the exercises conscientiously, you will have removed the causes of nervousness. Nervous energy will then be your servant and not your master, just as the gears are to the experienced driver, or electric current is to the electrician. To convince you on this point, which is so important, let us analyse each of the six causes of Fear and see if you have mastered them.

1. *Fear of the Unknown.*

This fear springs from two sources, ignorance of the technique of speaking and unfamiliarity with the actual delivery, and its removal depends on a study of the science of the mind, and practice in the art of delivery. Thanks to the popular misconception that training is unnecessary for speakers and that all that is required is some knowledge, the glib use of words, and the pluck to face an audience, many speakers are lulled by a false sense of security into undertaking a task for which they are unqualified. The moment they face an audience they experience a sense of responsibility, which arouses their critical faculties and they are overwhelmed by the sudden consciousness that they are handling a powerful force about which they know little or nothing. The result is Fear which takes control of their nervous system and puts their mental gears into reverse, with the consequence that uncontrolled or maladjusted nerves cause disastrous physical consequences and often sheer panic. Fumbling, readjustment, or rigid self-control may avoid catastrophe, but nervous exhaustion will result, and a promising speaker may be plunged into the slough of despond, possibly never to emerge. The result would be exactly the same if a rash singer attempted concert work without any voice training, and few stage artists would be given an important part without some training in the technique of their trade. Why should speakers be in a different category when their task is further complicated by the creation, as well as the expression of ideas. No wonder that the subconscious mind is appalled by the task with which it is confronted and realizes too late that knowledge must be co-ordinated, words skilfully handled, and that the so-called pluck is mere brazen impudence.

This then is Fear No. 1 and a prime factor is nervousness which knowledge of technique will conquer even if you cannot put your knowledge into practice at the start.

To quote a Persian proverb: "He who knows not and knows that he knows not is a child, teach him. He that knows and knows that he knows is a sage, follow him." You will be a child until you know your technique, and rightly nervous until you have gained confidence by practice, but one or two successful speeches, properly prepared and delivered, will give you confidence, and when you know that you know you will be a sage and will no longer fear the unknown.

2. *Fear of being Misunderstood.*

A creative mind intent on conveying a message is afraid that the message will not register as intended, and can only be reassured by a reasoned plan, notes, or some effective mind direction. If this is not available, muddled ideas become mental stammering and Fear assumes control, driving its unhappy victim to repeat the same point *ad nauseam* instead of moving on swiftly and smoothly to the next stage. Speeches planned on sound architectural lines with helpful notes will remove this fear, just as study of a map beforehand, or knowledge of the route, will prevent a motorist pulling up at every crossroads, and will enable him to move on swiftly and surely with an easy mind.

3. *Fear of the Audience.*

Skill in handling audiences is a matter of psychology and a very important aspect of speaking. At the start of a meeting, there is always an intangible barrier between the speaker and the listener (another form of fear of the unknown) and this produces nervousness in any sensitive speaker. Learn to tune in as recommended in Chapter 5 and this fear will vanish. Adjustment to audiences responds to the same rules as adjustment to life, and courage, cheerfulness, tact, patience, and imagination will work wonders.

4. Fear of being Inaudible.

Learn to handle the tools of your trade, especially the use of your lips, tongue, teeth, jaw, and the roof of your mouth. The expert has a sure touch and knows he can rely on his skill so has no fear of failure, but the amateur who has not learnt his trade is highly nervous and voice conscious all the time. Satisfy yourself beforehand that your voice is adequate for the job, and forget it when speaking, so that your mind can relax and concentrate on ideas. Sometimes the sound of your own voice is frightening when listened to consciously for the first time, so remove this fear by speaking aloud and making friends with it.

5. Fear of Oneself.

Modesty which conjures up imaginary faults, conceit which is concerned with the effect on the audience, or imagination which pictures an all-knowing questioner in the audience can release this Fear and create nervousness. Mental concentration is the weapon to slay it, as a mind which is absorbed in developing an interesting argument will not be distracted by these fanciful ideas.

6. Fear of Physical Reaction.

The first plunge into public speaking often reveals quite unexpectedly the physical strain imposed on the nervous system. Muscles controlling your lungs, your body, or your memory may need strengthening, mannerisms which divert physical energy may need checking, deep breathing may have to be practised, but once you are aware of these necessary adjuncts to speaking you can overhaul the machinery and be reasonably confident of withstanding the strain. The human machine, like all machinery, breaks down occasionally and bad health or brain tiredness will react on your speaking ability, but just as no healthy minded person should live in constant fear of illness, so no trained speaker should anticipate physical breakdowns. Should mental blackouts occur, it is not necessarily a tragedy, and auto-suggestion can be practised, or methods of diverting audiences can be learnt, or appeal by a frank confession of your mental lapse can be tried. Any of these remedies can overcome Fear and restore self-confidence.

Here then are the six Giants of Fear which cause nervousness and you will find that the Right Way Method has supplied you with the weapons with which to conquer them.

1. Fear of the Unknown conquered by knowledge of technique and practice.

2. Fear of muddled ideas conquered by clear mind direction and good notes.

3. Fear of the audience conquered by study of psychology.

4. Fear of inaudibility conquered by good voice production.

5. Fear of oneself by concentration and memory training.

6. Fear of physical strain conquered by deep breathing and physical adjustment.

Accept the challenge of Nervousness gladly and confidently, try out your Right Way weapons and banish these Fears forever. Take courage from the knowledge that many noted orators such as Demosthenes – Pitt – Disraeli – Roosevelt and Churchill suffered agonies of nervousness, but having conquered the Fear that inspired it, they released controlled nervous energy with results that made History.

9

Delivery

Four Essentials to Success

The Art of Delivery is of supreme importance to singers and actors who get their voices to interpret the ideas of others because they get no help from the natural driving force of their own ideas and so have to study voice production, elocution, and the right use of gestures to ensure maximum efficiency. Their field of achievement is limited to individual interpretation, which is actually a subsidiary rôle, and so delivery is magnified in importance until the interpreter is often considered greater than the genius behind the words. How seldom does an audience remember the genius of Shakespeare when applauding the magnificently produced voice and the superb gestures of a great Shakespearian actor. The same is largely true of barristers, though they have greater scope as they can choose their own words, but their briefs are prepared by solicitors, who are seldom given credit for the ideas, which after all, were the basis of the winning arguments, though eloquence and skill were necessary for their presentation.

Speakers then who are merely the mouthpiece for the ideas of other brains, must master the art of Delivery which gives them power to stimulate feeling, so that artificial speech sounds natural without the inspiration of ideas, but clergymen and speakers who prepare their own subject matter are in a different category. Having produced the ideas, they have the compensating advantage of natural inspiration and mind control which should use their voices to the best advantage thus making Delivery a natural process rather than an acquired Art.

For this reason I do not propose to deal with voice production which is a deep and complex subject best left to experts, but will confine myself to the four essentials for public speaking, namely co-ordination of brain and voice, correct use of the mechanics of speech, proper stance and the absence of mannerisms, and an adequate vocabulary. Co-ordination of brain and voice result from mind training, the correct use of your voice you have probably acquired already for normal purposes, proper stance and absence of mannerisms will come with self-mastery and experience, and an adequate vocabulary is a matter of education. Test yourself to make sure that you possess these four essentials, and when satisfied, forget your voice, and use it as the automatic servant it was intended to be, rather than an intricate machine to be skilfully handled. It will then be natural and express your personality, whereas attempts to change it will set up disharmony in your mind make you self-conscious and may produce such horrors as the "refaned" voice, or an Oxford accent superimposed on a natural soft brogue or dialect.

If you are dissatisfied with your self-analysis, see if your voice is flat, hesitant, toneless or lacking in inflection; if so, study the following notes on co-ordination of brain and voice. Should your voice be breathless, thin and lacking in tone, slurred or mumbling, then you are using your lungs, lips, teeth, tongue, or jaw incorrectly, and must diagnose your trouble and apply the appropriate remedy. A composer must train his fingers to interpret music on an instrument but he masters scales and acquires the necessary skill by wisely training with a qualified teacher, quite apart from his creative work, so that he will not be frustrated by inadequate presentation of his ideas, or be dependent on an interpreter. In the same way, a speaker requires mastery of the mechanism of the voice, but this is a separate branch of speech training which I prefer to leave to experts.

Readers who use their voice correctly in normal conversation can trust it to respond adequately in speech making. They are advised however to check it and gain confidence by a periodical overhaul. The hints given overleaf may be all they require but they are obvious and elementary and where speech defects are revealed, readers are advised to study one of the many books on voice production (there are dozens of specialist titles, many written with the acting profession in mind, available from bookshops or libraries).

Mannerisms are irritating and affect the speaker's mental concentration and the audience, so they are dealt with in this chapter, but words have a chapter to themselves. As all speakers must be satisfied that they possess the four essentials to good delivery already mentioned, let us check them once again.

1. Co-ordination of Brain and Voice

If you are interested in this book, and agree with the main thesis that natural speech entails feeling, directing control of the voice through reason, you will know that any picture conjured up in the mind will be reproduced in the voice, and thence transmitted to the minds of listeners. The more vivid the picture, and the deeper the emotion, the clearer will be the transmission, and the more accurately will you vibrate the right note on your vocal chords. Imagine the five registers of your voice – your deep chest notes, your normal speaking voice through your lips, your nasal intonation, or your high pitched exciting tones which seem to come through your forehead or the top of your head. Now try to make your mind cry, reflect, whisper, or dream by conjuring up some sad, serious, or confidential idea, concentrate on this idea and then try expressing it aloud, and note the automatic use of your deep register and your confidential tone because Nature intended low-pitched tones for serious reflection. Repeat the following, thinking of the idea behind the sentence

(*Sad*)	The eyes of a dog sitting by its dead master ...
	A cemetery makes one think ...
(*Serious*)	The atomic bomb was a shattering discovery ...
	The sum total of human misery in the world ...
(*Dreaming*)	Escape to the land of one's dreams is one of the precious freedoms still left.
	I saw a vision of what might have been.

(*Whispering*) In confidence let me whisper ...

If spoken naturally, all these sentences should register in low tones, and if you try repeating them in a high-pitched voice, you will realize how difficult it is and how ridiculous the results.

Now try picturing something amusing, or exciting, or alive with movement, and express it naturally. The appropriate words will automatically use the higher and lighter tones of your voice. Try the following sentences.

(*Amusing*)   A hearty laugh rang out and pealed through the rafters.
His grin reached from ear to ear.

(*Exciting*)   Life is a thrilling adventure.
A marvellous discovery.

(*Alive*)   The lark soared upwards.
The thought of foamy, frothy beer increased his pace from a leisurely stroll to a run.

You have now proved for yourself that the emotion in your mind controls the inflection and tone of your voice, but this emotion must be released if it is to do its work properly, and the sincerity with which you try to express it will control your wise use of words and your selection of appropriate gestures.

Another controlling factor affecting your voice is your conception of your audience. Just as your emotions affected your tone and pitch, so the picture in your mind of your listener will decide the emphasis in your voice, and the words most likely to convince him. Ignorant minds suggest force to bludgeon them into acceptance of ideas, and you will emphasize by forceful words – greater voice volume, and emphatic gestures. Intelligent and knowledgeable minds, on the other hand, will appreciate wit, subtlety, and rapier-like methods, and you will automatically use appeal, humour, and persuasion with their appropriate tones, words, and gestures.

If mind direction is the source of expressive voices and vibrant tones it is obvious that lack of mind control is the cause of *flat* voices. You will get flatness therefore if your creative mind is disinterested, and therefore inactive, or if some obstruction is preventing the mind direction from reaching and controlling the voice.

A disinterested mind is usually the result of making a speech based round ideas which are not its own, and the voice is flat, unless conscious artificial use of it is introduced. Again lack of interest can come from over-familiarity with its own ideas, as in the case of the same speech delivered too frequently, and here the remedy is new frames, or illustration, for the same facts. Another cause of mind disinterest is failure to grasp the meaning of words not of its own choosing, such as reading of a report for the first time. Pre-digestion of the contents will often stimulate interest, and add more colour to the voice. There is a noticeable difference between the intelligent reading of a lesson in church, when the reader has been over it previously and is moved by the words, the meaning of which has been grasped, and the meaningless gabble of the disinterested reader, whose thoughts are not on his words, or whose mind cannot grasp the meaning quickly enough, and whose natural gestures are thwarted by having to hold and turn over pages and keep the eyes directed on the written word.

The second cause of absent mind-control, *i.e.* when creative ideas provide the impulse, but that impulse fails to reach and colour the voice, is usually found in memorized speeches. The efforts of the mechanical mind to recall the exact words memorized stifles the natural stimulus which depends on the free choice of words for effective voice-control.

To sum up – a flat voice is the result of absence of direct control by feeling, and is most often found in second-hand, read, or memorized speeches so these should be avoided when relying on the natural use of the voice. If such speeches are necessary the art of delivery must be carefully studied, and consciously employed.

Another fault arising from lack of co-ordination between brain and voice is the *hesitant* voice. In this case, there is delay in propelling the idea forward for expression, owing to absence of a clear plan. It is really mental stammering, and the cure is to be found in notes, as a glance at them should immediately propel the idea into position for contacting the voice. Alternatively, failing to focus ideas quickly enough may lead to verbosity, as meaningless, and therefore colourless words are used to fill the painful gap.

If the creative mind is completely divorced from the voice, and reason has been by-passed, the voice can be used by the mechanical mind with amazing results, such as Spoonerisms. On one occasion Spooner was asked what luggage he required for a journey, and is reputed to have replied "Two bugs and a rag" instead of two bags and a rug. Presumably Spooner's thoughts were on weightier matters, and his mechanical mind was in control.

2. CORRECT USE OF THE VOICE

Few children are taught the correct use of the voice and their ability to speak attractively is often a matter of luck in their environment or the associates whose speech they copy. All should be taught the miracle of the human voice, its uses and its powers, and the various functions of the lungs, throat, jaw, tongue, lips, and teeth. Those who have never produced their voices correctly, and who now realize the necessity for doing so if they hope to achieve success as speakers, or indeed in any sphere of life, are advised to take a course of training with any qualified teacher of voice production, and they will learn how to breathe, how to model words and how to project them. It is a long job requiring patience and practice.

A speaker must remember that the *voice* follows the *eyes* so fix your gaze on some spot about 18 to 24 inches above the heads of those in the back row to get initial voice projection. Later on, as you relax, you will doubtless look at various sections of your audience more directly, but it is as well to re-orient your eyes from time to time to the spot originally selected to counteract the fatal attraction of the one outstanding face which invites undue attention because it is stimulating and arresting!

A controlled, dignified start gives initial confidence so decide on an easy position and take it up as naturally as a golfer addresses a ball or a pianist raises his music stool.

A breathless voice which gives a feeling of insecurity to the speaker, and weakens the confidence of the audience, can be checked quite easily.

A thin weak voice is often the result of tightening the vocal chords at the back of the throat, and full round vowel sounds such as A – Oh – Ah should be practised.

Bad articulation is a frequent fault with lazy speakers who do not trouble to use their lips, tongue or teeth correctly, often failing to open their lips, or teeth, and so murdering their words by strangulation. The tongue often gets in the way of the sound coming from an open throat, or again a speaker may fail to project his voice forward sufficiently to enable it to carry to the back of a big hall.

Inaudibility is often due to clipping words, such as dropping the final "g" or running words into each other. Check your prefixes and suffixes as clear-cut beginnings and endings have carrying power.

Test articulation by asking a friend to stand some distance away and repeat:

A nice man.
An ice man.

A diseased man.
A deceased man.

Are they wise mice?
Are they nice mice?

If the different meanings were not quite clear the first time, say the words slowly, and analyse the different movements of the tongue and lips so as to impress on your mind the need for care in differentiating one from the other.

Experiment with your voice, learn its power and how to pitch it. Once you are satisfied that the mechanism for producing satisfactory sound is working smoothly, forget it, and rely on your creative mind to use this sound to the best advantage. Correct superficial faults when you have discovered them, but get expert help if in any doubt and if there is any deep-seated trouble.

3. STANCE AND MANNERISMS

The right way to stand should result from correct breathing, but bodily health affects your natural stance, and excessive smoking, eating or drinking, tiredness, or reliance on the backs of chairs, or the edge of tables, weakens mental concentration and impairs mind direction, with consequent deterioration in the quality of your voice.

Any mannerisms are bad, as your mind has the dual task of controlling physical movements as well as concentrating on ideas, and it is easy to become a slave to some irritating habit, such as walking about a platform, twiddling with a pencil, or standing on one foot. Any mannerisms which prevent the free use of your hands for natural gestures affect your voice, as your mind is temporarily impeded in its work of directing the voice, by a feeling of frustration because the intended gesture was not forthcoming.

10

Words

As Samuel Johnson said, "Words are the clothes of thought" and, like clothes, your speech can be vivid or drab, streamlined or clumsy, trim or fussy, attractive or dowdy, according to the use you make of words which are both the material and the tools for cutting and fitting the dress in which you finally clothe your speech.

Nobody can do good work with bad tools, yet how often do speakers use worn-out tools, *i.e.* hackneyed words; blunt tools, *i.e.* inapt, offensive words; and rusty tools, *i.e.* beautiful words which are dull and fail to reflect their real beauty because speakers are unfamiliar with them and misuse them.

Surely it is a crime to murder or mutilate our glorious language, yet how little help is given to speakers in the choice and use of their material and tools compared with the time devoted to training a dress designer, artist, cutter or fitter.

Ideas and words are interdependent and create each other, and the knowledge that you are limiting the creation and expression of ideas to the extent of your vocabulary should spur you on to the study and mastery of words. Effective speech depends on clear thinking which focuses ideas and then opens the mind to a natural flow of words which picks up the ideas and carries them forward through the mouth in a smooth, effortless stream. The volume is controlled by the number and magnitude of the ideas to be covered and is automatic provided there are adequate reserves of words available, but how many speakers have experienced the anguish of feeling fine ideas die at birth because they were not immediately clothed in warm, comfortable, suitable words.

Apart from fear of "drying up", which is a very potent cause of nervousness, failure to find words readily saps confidence by slowing down speech, as the filling of a basin is slowed down when the tap only yields a slow trickle or a drop at a time. Equally, failure to turn off the supply would cause a devastating overflow; so supply and control are both necessary.

To ensure a smooth flow of words available at all times you need adequate reserves of dignified, beautiful, forceful and pleasing words, so overhaul your supply. Minds store words mechanically and we all know far more words than we use, but lazy minds pick surface words to save trouble and never pause to ask whether they are drab or musty – hence the shoddy material unworthy of good workmanship. Increase your stock of single words, then pair them up and group them and ring the changes by familiarizing yourself with synonyms, alternatives and associated words.

SINGLE WORDS AND PAIRS

Every complete sentence contains a noun or pronoun and a verb, and these are pivotal words clothed by adjectives and adverbs to colour and qualify them.

A good exercise to show you the range and power of adjectives is to put down six nouns, *e.g.* speech, music, food, newspaper, garden, or house; select one in which you are interested and make a list of twenty-four appropriate adjectives picked at random from your store. You will probably think of far more, but if you cannot think of twenty-four for any of these nouns your stock is definitely inadequate, and you must take steps to increase it. Do not fly to a dictionary, as your own ideas require your own words to do them justice and produce them naturally, and the value of this exercise is to make you overhaul and list your own stock before adding to or replacing it. Divide your adjectives into those expressing approval and disapproval. You will probably find it easier to do the latter first as destructive words spring to most minds more readily, especially when the critical faculty is uppermost as it must be for effective training.

Having made these two lists, analyse them and group the adjectives in the same way that you have learned to group ideas in building up your speech, so that you can regulate the temperature, volume and density of your adjectives at will.

General adjectives are the overall words, used most often, as they give a quick, comprehensive picture; other associated groups are more selective and chosen to qualify and stress various outstanding features.

Try this exercise on the noun "speech" and compare your result with the following example.

Noun: Speech

Adjectives grouped from list made at random:

Group.	Condemnatory.	Group.	Approving.
1. General	Bad. Atrocious. Appalling. Ineffective. Ghastly. Futile.	1. General	Good. Effective. Convincing. Clear. Grand. Excellent.
2. Describing an Ineffective Speech.	Vague. Flabby. Incoherent. Monotonous. Colourless. Lifeless.	2. Describing a Pleasing Speech.	Beautiful. Colourful. Expressive. Well-delivered. Sympathetic. Audible.
3. Describing an Irritating Speech.	Inaudible. Hesitant. Verbose. Irrelevant. Laboured. Inconsequent.	3. Describing an Understandable Speech.	Lucid. Concise. Informative. Direct. Convincing. Logical.
4. Describing a Hurtful Speech.	Sardonic. Bitter. Ironical. Slanderous. Malicious. Scurrilous.	4. Describing an Inspiring Speech.	Dynamic. Enthralling. Stimulating. Moving. Forceful. Sparkling.

Having classified your adjectives in any groups you please, now link up with memory by recalling a good and then a bad speech which you have heard, and describe with appropriate adjectives taken from different groups. You will probably need one general and one qualifying adjective. *e.g.*:

It was a grand, moving speech.
It was an atrocious, scurrilous speech.

You have thus linked your adjectives and noun into a word picture which you can then compare with the true picture which memory flashed on your mental screen. Adjectives are intoxicating, so strict control is necessary but remember black and white is not the only medium in which art is expressed and you should know the value of glowing colours, pastel shades, oils and water colours; in other words you have not attained speech mastery until you can colour, heat, cool and regulate your words.

Before turning to ways of increasing vocabulary, let us pursue this exercise a bit further, as so far you have only touched the obvious words in your vocabulary.

If you have given time and the necessary mental concentration to this exercise, many more adjectives than the forty-eight in your groups will have occurred to you, as every word suggests further words, so to register the surplus words effectively, do a quick exercise. Take each letter of the alphabet and write down an adjective describing speech – which you have not already used. My alphabet is as follows:

A	Academic.	N	Nauseating.
B	Bucolic.	O	Odious.
C	Crude.	P	Pugnacious.
D	Diplomatic.	Q	Querulous.
E	Erudite.	R	Raucous.
F	Fantastic.	S	Sincere.
G	Gracious.	T	Terrifying.
H	High-minded.	U	Unctuous.
I	Ignoble.	V	Vivacious.
J	Jocular.	W	Wonderful.
K	Kindly.	X	Xanthic.
L	Lamentable.	Y	Youthful.
M	Mortifying.	Z	Zealous.

I admit I had to refer to a dictionary for X, and found Xanthic meant "appertaining to yellow", which seemed appropriate to some speeches! All the other words should be familiar as they have common usage, but applying them to a particular noun helps to group them in your mind for easy, effortless release.

By the time you have tried this exercise on the other five nouns in your original list, you will have surprised yourself with the power and range of the adjectives stored in your mind, and if you have been caught by the lure of words you can continue to chase them by replacing each adjective by a synonym expressing the same meaning, or an associated word which would do as an alternative, or an antonym to link up opposites. The same exercise can be applied to verbs and adverbs.

When you are thoroughly familiar with your adjectives and adverbs and can handle them expertly, linking adjectives to nouns and adverbs to verbs quickly and intelligently, remember the rusty tools and keep your words bright by practice, not as a task but as a hobby to be done at odd moments. Harness your powers of observation and your imagination, *e.g.* when you are strolling round a garden, imagine you are describing the flowers to a blinded ex-gardener, and think of appropriate vivid words, alternating between stately flowers such as delphiniums and small delicate flowers such as snowdrops, by way of contrast.

Before leaving the study of words, test your ability to pair up words in an original way. Make a list of hackneyed pairs such as.

stony silence.   perilous adventure.
dejected appearance.   headline news.

and ring the change on both adjectives and nouns. You may coin some vivid phrases which will appeal to your mind forcibly and so occur to you spontaneously when speaking, thus projecting your personality into your speech. Churchill was a past master of wedded words and opposites, and gave us an outstanding example in his plea to Parliament "... not to let the *soaring eagles* be brought down by the *squawking parrots* when the *clear thinking of war unity* has been replaced by the *turgid stream of post-war discord*".

GROUPS OF WORDS

After pairs, clearly defined groups of words are the next essential of the well-equipped speaker, and groups of synonyms and alternatives are the most useful.

Synonyms.
You have already practised single synonyms, but most

key words can be amplified into a group. These groups can be obtained from a dictionary but are retained and used more readily if compiled by yourself.

Pick a certain number of adjectives from the lists appertaining to Speech, such as flabby, clumsy, vague, ordinary, slangy, beautiful, expressive, vivid, exciting, stimulating and descriptive, and add five or six similar words to each one. This will give you a group of synonyms for each adjective and provide a wide range of words to express exact shades of meaning.

Alternatives.

A good way to find alternative words is to group them under key ideas as illustrated below:

Ideas and their Relative Words

SEEING.
  Eye.
  Vision.
  Watchfulness.
  Observing.
  Noting.
  Recording.

UNITY.
  Partner.
  Marriage.
  Federation.
  Corporate body.
  Membership.
  Enrolment.

PASSAGE.
  Opening.
  Path.
  Road.
  Steps.
  Lane.
  Byeway.

ORDER.
  Neatness.
  Accuracy.
  Skill.
  Excellence.
  Tidiness.
  Precision.

TAKING.
  Seize.
  Acquire.
  Accept.
  Achieve.
  Steal.
  Appropriate.

SOUND.
  Speech.
  Singing.
  Laughter.
  Melody.
  Noise.
  Music.

Having compiled your groups of synonyms and alternatives, test your own speech. If you find yourself using a word such as "unquestionably" too often, make a group of alternatives such as "infallibly", "irrefutably", "indubitably" or "definitely", for variety. Aim at descriptive words rather than fine words. A speaker can be more trite than a writer, because what is obvious to the intelligent reader is not necessarily obvious to everybody in an audience consisting of minds possibly ranging from half-wits to experts.

General Groups.

Some minds like alliterations (though this is a pernicious habit) and would enjoy making lists of people, animals or articles beginning with the same letter, or composing telegrams of words, *e.g.* "D" for "Speech":

Dyke, Dymchurch,
Delivered dynamic discourse during discussion.
Disastrous denouement developed. Deeply disgraced.
Dick.

Groups of words altered by prefixes and suffixes are also useful, such words beginning with "pre" or ending with "ing".

Word grouping is invaluable for children and should be included in school curricula. Crosswords could also be encouraged, especially making as well as solving them, and word exercises such as taking a page of a dictionary and marking:

(*a*) Words known and used.
(*b*) Words known but not used.
(*c*) Words unknown.

ENLARGING YOUR VOCABULARY

This can best be done by reading good verse or prose, but the lesson will only be learnt if you note words that appeal to you, by underlining them or noting them mentally and copying them out on second reading. Having picked them out, analyse each word separately and trace its source of appeal. What emotion did it arouse? Did it inspire, soothe, charm, anger, or merely appeal by its clarity?

Having decided the particular merit of each word, you will have grasped the emotional power of words and taught your mind to be selective. Doctors and nurses who deal with road casualties soon realize the balm of soothing words, particularly in the first moments of shock and pain, as a preparation to practical and possibly painful treatment. It is as well, therefore, to have an ample supply of soothing, inspiring, sweet and nourishing words as well as the salt, seasoning and spice.

When you have probed the weak sections of your vocabulary you can strengthen them by more objective reading.

If you are deficient in weighty words, pregnant with meaning, read the essays of Emerson or Macaulay. If you decide that your speech is too abrupt and harsh and that you need more harmony in your phrasing, try poetry or the smooth, majestic, rolling words of the Proverbs or the Psalms. If you lack subtlety, wit and humour, turn to Bernard Shaw or A. P. Herbert, or for clear-cut meanings study the old writers such as Plato, Aristotle and Cicero. The latter were content to take their readers by the shortest and most direct route to a given point, unlike so many modern writers who seem more intent on losing their readers by taking them through a mental maze with high hedges of words obscuring points.

These are only a few suggestions for the study of words, as the field is vast and the choice must be your own. Like the use of the voice, words are a separate branch of speech training, and time spent on it will repay you a thousandfold.

Do not think you must have a big library, for, though this is a great help, one volume of Shakespeare would provide all the answers if the reading were purposeful. Pick out a few words each week-end and make a conscious effort to introduce them into your conversation during the coming week. At first you will hesitate, and the timid, unenterprising mind may fall back on the old familiar words, but persevere and after one or two attempts you will enjoy the experiment and find fresh inspiration and colouring.

It is inadvisable to try new words in a speech, as fear of mispronunciation will cause your mind to hesitate, and deaden your voice. Overcome this fear previously in conversation and you will enjoy a feeling of triumphant achievement when you first use the word easily and naturally in a speech.

Reading biographies enables one to see into the workings of other minds and so stimulates thought. It also helps you to form a philosophy of life which is the background of speeches, for natural speech portrays character. Cicero tells us that the perfect orator is the perfect man.

One could devote a volume to the selection and power of words, so often wrongly used to fill a vacuum, drown a meaning, intoxicate a speaker or stun an audience.

Their real use is to provide wings to carry ideas swiftly and by the most direct route (as the bird flies) into the hearts and minds of listeners, so use them wisely and sparingly, assured of their suitability and conscious of their power. As money is a symbol of wealth, so words are the symbol of a rich mind. The love, admiration, reverence and awe which they inspire are aptly expressed in the words of Richard Church, with which I close this chapter.

THESE WORDS

These daily words you listen to are not
One man's invention, but the growth of time,
Seeded from nobility and crime.
Some are blemished fruits, destined to rot
And fall. Some revive that were forgot.
A few, like death in life, may faintly chime
Dropped from the belfry of a poet's rhyme
Upon the graves in history's burial plot.
But all of them, long lived or quickly gone,
Are active powers, the radium of thought,
The close-packed atoms of our human story.
Here then is need for caution. Be admonished
To use these daily words as though God-wrought
Magical master keys to light and glory.

11

Phraseology

If words are the material with which you cover ideas, the use of them decides the cut and style of clothes and you will naturally choose your own design, but obviously knowledge of grammar, pruning and meanings of words are basic requirements.

1. GRAMMAR

Every speaker should have a sound knowledge of grammar, and use correct grammar automatically. We are usually taught so inadequately at school, that many books are deemed necessary for the help of writers in later life, but there is not one, as far as I know, designed primarily for speakers.

Presumably speakers are supposed to follow the same rules, yet the technique of speaking and writing are completely different. The writer can select and change words at leisure, whereas the speaker relies for effect on quick reactions to ideas and must find the apt word which will not only satisfy reason but will convey feeling by the right intonation and the right context. His is the difficult task of producing a lightning sketch of a vivid idea in colourful words.

The aim of a speaker is to impress listeners with *what* is said rather than *how* it is said, therefore correct grammar must be automatic as there is no time to consider it, and a speaker may be forgiven if his enthusiasm at times ignores the rules which the creative mind considers subsidiary to the ideas conveyed and which reason has not time to check too carefully.

I am not suggesting that you should speak ungrammatically, but the force of an idea and the sincerity of the speaker will cover many minor faults, and if split

infinitives, abhorrent to some writers, slip out occasionally, do not worry unduly as you will be in the company
of many great speakers. Forceful speakers often find it
easier to emphasize *before* a verb than *after* it, for instance, "To grimly survey an audience" seems to accent-
uate the grimness better than the correct sentence "To
survey an audience grimly", and few in the audience
would notice the fault, but be careful if reporters are
present as a verbatim report read in the paper the next
day might be a blow to one's self-respect.

A common fault is the misuse of "will" and "shall"
and the Irish are particularly prone to this mistake. I
speak with feeling, as it took me years to grasp the error
of the sentence which I was made to write out at school:
"I *will* drown and nobody shall save me". I have since
discovered that in speaking I can make "will" sound like
"shall" and vice versa, so I have ceased to worry and have
had no unflattering comments, which may comfort other
speakers who feel their grammar is shaky.

Experience has taught me that there are three rules
which speakers ignore at their peril:

(*a*) Placing relative words near their subject.

(*b*) Separating subsidiary ideas by mental punctuation.

(*c*) Correct use of pauses.

(a) Relative Words.
Having focused your main idea, train your mind to put
relative words as near as possible. Efficient speaking is
clear speaking, and if you mean what you say and say
what you mean you must take the most direct route.
Devious routes are often chosen deliberately for vagueness, and nothing confuses listeners more than the introduction of subsidiary ideas before the main point has
registered. A classic example of this fault is the following
advertisement:

"Sale of piano by lady with carved legs."

A rambling speaker might confuse the issue still more
by following the secondary train of thought, that is,
"the lady" and adding "giving up house" before com-

pleting the details of the piano. The sentence would then be:

"Sale of piano by lady giving up house with carved legs." and we would then have to decide if the carved legs applied to the lady, the house or the piano. "Sale of piano with carved legs" must *precede* any qualifying remarks in the interest of lucidity.

(b) Mental Punctuation.

This follows the same rules as written punctuation, but is helped by the intonation of the voice.

If you saw the following sentence written without punctuation it would seem quite unintelligible and the result would be just the same if spoken without a pause:

I say John I hear say that you say that I say I say at every word that I say I say John. Now John if I do say I say at every word that I say I say John that is no reason why you should say that I say I say at every word that I say I say John.

Now repeat it aloud, pausing at every comma and emphasizing every word italicized, and it will make sense.

I *say* John, I hear say, that *you* say that I say, "*I say*", at *every* word that I say, I say John. *Now*, John, if I *do* say, "*I say*", at every word that I say, I say John, this is *no reason* why *you* should say that I say "*I say*" at every word that I say, I say John.

The different inflection of the voice for the "I say" in inverted commas, shows that this is a superfluous interjection and makes the meaning as clear as it could be in such a ridiculous sentence.

(c) Pauses.

There are many kinds of pauses, rhetorical, dramatic, and lung-filling, and many faults develop as a result of neglecting one of the most valuable adjuncts of a speaker.

Rhetorical pauses keep the attention of an audience; dramatic pauses spotlight strong points, and lung-filling pauses are essential to smooth delivery.

Quick thinkers often leave their sentences incomplete because their minds are racing ahead of their tongues, or, worse still, use the wrong word because they are concentrating on the next point and the wrong word is supplied automatically. Train your mind to complete a sentence and pause to refill your lungs, which will give you time to focus the next point and select appropriate words.

Again, slurred words and misuse of your tongue are often due to the fact that there is not time to re-adjust your articulatory organs between sentences, so do not *fear* pauses, *use* them effectively.

2. PRUNING

A pruning knife and the skill to use it wisely should be the prized possession of any speaker, and of the two faults, multiplication and parsimony in the use of words, the former is the more detrimental to clear speech.

Many examples can be found in legal phraseology which may be necessary for lawyers trying to block holes for foxy criminals, but it is deplorable in speakers. The following is a good illustration which appeared in the *Public Speaker,* a paper which has long since passed away.

Plain question – plain answer.
Solicitor: Now Sir, did you or did you not, on the date in question, or at any time previously or subsequently, say, or even intimate, to the defendant or anyone else, whether friend or mere acquaintance, or, in fact, a stranger, that the statement imputed to you, whether just or unjust, and denied by the plaintiff, was a matter of no moment or other? Answer, did you or did you not?
Witness: Did I or did I not what?

Readers are invited to give a précis of the solicitor's remarks in twelve or eighteen words and to practise condensing their own and other people's speeches until they learn the art of streamlining.

A recent speech I heard began as follows:

"We all regret the position that has arisen in regard to the difficulty of finding markets overseas. There are many factors, but one, which is recognized on all sides, is the high cost of production."

Here you have thirty-five words which could have been reduced to sixteen, as follows:

"A regrettable fact is the shrinkage of world markets
owing, chiefly, to high costs of production"

and the audience would have grasped the point far more
quickly. Brief, clear, simple sentences are easier to say,
easier to understand, and far more dramatic. One of my
most vivid war-time recollections illustrates this point.
It was the day France fell, and the B.B.C. announcement
was as follows:

"The position in regard to France is serious."

Later in the day Churchill announced in the Commons:

"The news from France is very bad."

Contrast the two statements. Something described as
"serious" is capable of a dozen different interpretations
according to the temperament of the listener, but there
is no ambiguity about the plain statement, "very bad".

Understatement can, of course, be overdone and starve
a speech, a fault to which the unemotional Britisher is
prone. Stories of this type are legion; one I can remember,
which is typical, concerns two men gazing at a magni-
ficent sunset. One said, "Not so dusty, what?" and the
other replied, "Well, you need not rave about it like a
poet, need you, old man?"

Cover the bones of your argument with adequate flesh,
but avoid both over- and under-statement. To do this
requires a knowledge of the true value of each word.

3. Meanings of Words

Even superficial study of the meanings of words reveals
that few words have a precise universal meaning, as each
user interprets them differently according to the idea to
be conveyed. Such variations are introduced by voice inflections or different contexts. Again, words can alter
their meaning by common usuage or by blatant misuse.

Take the word "democracy", for example; so many
interpretations have been given to it that the U.S.A.,
Russia and Great Britain all claim to have a "demo-
cratic" government, though such governments range from
"free" capitalism to iron-bound dictatorship.

Many words have diverged from their original meanings, such as "fond", which meant "foolish", and "silly",
which meant "happy"; here is where dictionaries are
necessary, as they bring us back to original meanings.

Speakers have a wide choice of dictionaries, and Roget's *Thesaurus* is the best, but they also need a good standard dictionary and something like *Hartrampf's Vocabularies* (which groups key words with their associated words and synonyms).

For Discussion Group purposes in particular it is essential to agree on the exact definition of any subject under discussion.

The misuse of words is a real spiritual danger, as Socrates warned us, and the propagandists have proved it to our cost. When this is done deliberately it is the vilest form of debasing words of sterling worth. The speaker pays the price in ineffective delivery, but can, nevertheless, do untold harm by what is nothing more or less than word cheating.

Words are often used as a smoke-screen to hide unpleasant truths; thus politicians describe unsaleable goods as "frustrated exports", slacking becomes "working to rule", and incompetent muddlers, instead of being exposed, are branded as "well-meaning". One longs for the direct, robust language of Shakespeare instead of the vague anæmic speech of to-day. Too many have acquired the fatal facility of using words that imitate thought rather than creating and expressing it, and they should follow the good advice of Lord Vansittart, who headed an article:

"Think clearly, speak plainly, and mean it."

Bad grammar, muddled sentences, verbosity and the misuse of words can spoil a good speech as surely as badly cut, shoddy clothes can ruin a perfect figure. They are all pitfalls which a little thought and experience will teach you to avoid, and care should be taken to check yourself particularly when success invites slackness. Never allow your high standard of speaking to deteriorate; always remember that speech is too powerful, too dangerous, and too necessary to be handled lightly, and the care given to it should be in proportion to its value. Goethe places language on the pinnacle of all the human arts, and it is incontestably the highest gift that we possess.

12

Summing Up

The previous eleven chapters complete the Right Way Speech Training, but before summing up I would like to deal with a few minor points worth consideration, such as correct accent and emphasis, tactful education, eye magnetism, and consideration for audience.

ACCENT AND EMPHASIS

Accent on the wrong syllable is a frequent fault in speakers inexperienced in the use of words, and may bring smiles, or even ridicule from an audience, which shatters the self-confidence of any sensitive speaker. If in doubt study a dictionary showing the correct pronunciation, and if a word has a local pronunciation which is popular, though not necessarily correct, is is safer to give your audience what they like rather than leave the impression that you are trying to educate them.

The effect of emphasis on different words should be studied, as it can often change the whole meaning of a sentence. The following remark might be made by somebody meeting a friend who has failed to keep an appointment: "I stood at the crossroads as arranged". Such a sentence spoken naturally and without special emphasis on any word, would sound pleasant and allay hostility, but an aggrieved person might make it sound very different by stressing various words. Test yourself and you will find the result as follows: —

"I" emphasized, denotes personal grievance.

"stood" emphasized, suggests physical strain.

"crossroads" emphasized, infers exact meeting place.

"arranged" emphasized, conveys righteous indignation,

and smug satisfaction that the speaker is not to blame.

Repeat the sentence four times with the words stressed as suggested, analyse the effect, and you will have taught your mind a valuable lesson. A skilled speaker can convey a totally different meaning by emphasis, even when quoting exact words, and in expressing your own thought, the more different shades of meaning you can convey the more colourful will be your picture.

TACTFUL EDUCATION

Tactful education is essential for sympathetic consideration of your case. Never talk down to an audience, for though you are probably right to assume that the majority need the simplest point explained, the knowledgeable minority will resent the inference. Preface your remarks with "As you all know" and then proceed to tell them in case they have forgotten. You will achieve the same result and arouse no antagonism.

Much tactful education is done by analogies, but it is as well to check them and link them with points beforehand as spontaneous analogies can be surprisingly inappropriate! In one week I noted the following in speeches:

1. Bottlenecks must be ironed out.
2. The Atlantic must be bridged.
3. Work like beavers to clear the channels of thought.
4. Tempered steel must be added to the web of our negotiations with labour.

The first two are impossible, and the third ridiculous as beavers dam, not clear, channels. The last one, apart from being very stilted, is liable to misunderstanding as only a few in the audience would have any knowledge of steel webs, and to the majority the idea of introducing steel into anything as delicate as a spider's web would seem fantastic. Had the speaker said: "The quality of tempered steel must be added to our negotiations with labour" the meaning would have been plain to all.

EYE MAGNETISM

Few people realize the challenge of the human eye, but just as your voice follows your eye, so the latter reflects your ideas. Train your eye on the person to whom you are speaking and the compelling force of your creative mind, mirrored and intensified by your eyes, and co-ordinated with your voice, has a triple power like three searchlights synchronized into one powerful beam which must penetrate into the mind of your hearers. So strong is this magnetism of the eye, that a speaker can waken sleeping members of the audience by merely looking at them. (Nervous beginners should use this power with care and avoid direct eye contact with individuals, as if your gaze is returned and you get an equally powerful counter current, you may mesmerize each other, like a stoat with a rabbit, and find great difficulty in averting your gaze.)

Start by looking at fixed points in the centre, and on both sides of the hall above the heads of the audience, which will give the impression of looking at all in turn. Gradually as you gain confidence, look at each section of the audience in turn, picking out a friendly face for comfort or a hostile face for stimulation. Do not forget to turn to your Chairman occasionally as it is courteous to include him in your remarks and it is usually appreciated.

CONSIDERATION FOR THE AUDIENCE

Good speaking is a matter of good manners: that is, consideration for others, and the following suggestions would add to the comfort of the average audience:

1. *Think for them* by making your main points clear.
2. *Ease the transfer of thought* from one idea to another by means of link sentences.
3. *Air their memories* by repeating points instead of saying: "As I said" and leaving them to remember.
4. *Ease the strain of listening* by using apt, brief, simple words. Long words suggest snobbery, ignorance or laziness.
5. *Avoid irritating* by mumbling, mispronunciation, or constant repetition of a word, and above all by silly mannerisms.
6. *Gain friends* by humour and good temper and the use of words that express sympathy and understanding.

Consideration for one's audience seems a good note on which to finish, but before concluding let us check the various stages of training. The numbers correspond with the chapters of this book for reference purposes.

SUMMARY OF SPEECH TRAINING

Chapter 1	Studying natural speech and the mechanism of the mind controlling it.
Chapter 2	Extracting ideas from your creative mind which will have the driving force of emotions, such as enthusiasm, sincerity and interest.
Chapter 3	Harnessing Reason to creative ideas to provide planned objective. Acquired knowledge and trained intelligence direct thoughts to practical ends but must persuade rather than command or the creative mind will resent interference and disharmony will result.
Chapter 4	Note-making to aid reason. Memory training to recall creative ideas. Checking facts to give confidence.
Chapter 5	Tuning in to audiences, gaining and holding interest, driving home points, tact, statistics.
Chapter 6	Colouring and polishing of metaphors, illustrations, quotations. Repercussion of ideas.
Chapter 7	Filing facts. Recording impressions. Coining vivid phrases. Developing personality.
Chapter 8	Controlling nerves. Causes and mastery of nervousness.
Chapter 9	Harnessing voice to reason and imagination. Mind control of delivery. Faults and their cure.
Chapter 10	Power of words. Single words, pairs and groups. Adjectives, adverbs and word exercises.
Chapter 11	Phraseology and grammar. Pruning. Word meanings.
Chapter 12	Accents. Emphasis. Use of eyes. Comfort of Audience.

Conclusion

At last, the course is finished except for some hints on business, social, or political speeches, and the future lies in on your own hands. The Appendix on great speeches and their lessons should not be studied by beginners until they have perfected their own natural style, as they may be tempted to become mere copyists.

I hope you have had the courage and patience to persevere to the end and that results have proved to you the aptness of the title of this little book. You have only been told how to fashion and use the tools for your job, the choice of what you make with them is limitless, but you are equipped with the right tool for business, social, political, missionary, educational or family success, and practice alone will make you skilful in their use. Of course you will cut yourself, hurt others, blunt your tools, and possibly suffer agonies of fear at first though you should be less liable to nervousness after training, but early failure often leads to great success later.

To the young beginners, for whom this book is primarily intended, I would say that your inspiration should lie in the urgent need for a world that will satisfy your hidden longings, but how can you get it if you leave the fashioning of that world to others? Crystallize those secret longings into convincing, clear, brief speech, and you will be surprised at the welcome your ideas will receive. Most people realize that the pool of human understanding draws its strength from the wisdom of age, the vision of youth, the practical knowledge of experience, and the human emotions of the ordinary man and woman, and that each individual could, with advantages to all, contribute his or her quota.

Too long have we trusted the scientists, the politicians, and the social reformers, without supplying them with the material for their work in the shape of our own creative ideas. Let us bring forward these ideas, submit them to careful examination, and insist that what is worth while be given a trial. A mechanized world must be harnessed to a world of ideas, born in our creative minds, fashioned by reason and expressed by natural speech, if we are to drive through the clouds to the sunlight beyond. Ask yourself – Can I help in this great work?

SPEECHES FOR DIFFERENT OCCASIONS

Business Speeches.

These are usually governed by the rules of business procedure. It is unnecessary to tune-in and it is advisable to state your main arguments clearly and briefly at the start, develop them with the minimum of words and sum up forcibly at the end.

If great care is essential in dealing with subject matter, dictate the whole speech and revise, then write out main points on a card and try out the speech once or twice, noting the time taken in delivery. This will clarify your mind as to the order in which you intend to develop arguments, and still leave your mind a free choice of words rather than straining after memorized sentences.

Conduct of Meetings.

Readers wishing to learn meeting procedure are advised to study *The Right Way to Conduct Meetings, Conferences and Discussions** by A. G. Mears and J. M. Taylor. It is comprehensive and easy to follow. From the speaker's point of view the following suggestions may prove helpful:

1. *Chairman's opening remarks at a public meeting.*

This must be individual but a rough guide is to take points in the following order:

    (*a*) Welcome to audience.

    (*b*) Reference to local activities for inclusion in press report.

    (*c*) Record of speaker.

    (*d*) General reference to subject.

    (*e*) Appeal for quiet hearing (if necessary) and promise of question time after speech.

    (*f*) Formal introduction of speaker and his subject.

Maximum time is usually five minutes.

* A companion volume in the Paperfront Series. Uniform with this book.

2. Question time.

Insist on questions being addressed to the chair and appeal for brevity.

Do not allow more than one question at a time.

Ask those wishing to put questions to raise their hands and take them in the order in which this is done.

Call on questioner to stand and name next questioner so that he may be ready.

Repeat questions for benefit of those at the back of the hall if the speaker is willing that this should be done. It is not advisable to allow a weak chairman to do this as he may misinterpret the question and anger both questioner and speaker. On the other hand if done well it gives the speaker time to think out the answer, helps to translate dialects for the benefit of a visiting speaker and enables the chairman to answer purely local questions about which the speaker could know nothing.

3. Vote of Thanks.

Proposer should note points of exceptional interest in the speech, refer to them and link them up with his own remarks. This drives home main points, makes the speech relevant and pleases the speaker far more than personal adulation which becomes nauseating if it is done at too great length in order to fill the allotted time, usually about three minutes. Appreciation of the speaker should be the frame for appreciation of facts.

Seconders of vote of thanks usually confine themselves to formal seconding, and should endorse remarks of the proposer adding personal appreciation and finish with the words: "I have much pleasure, Mr. Chairman, in seconding the vote of thanks to our speaker so ably proposed by ——".

Political Speeches.

Appeal to emotion must precede facts with the average mixed audience, so care should be devoted to approaches and conclusions.

Written questions sent up beforehand are seldom popular as audiences suspect speakers of preparing them with answers attached. If the chairman is experienced, get him to repeat the question as this gives you time to think out the answer, enables those at the back to hear the question, and often clarifies it.

Hecklers are best treated as sincere enquirers, as a witty answer, though often effective, will make an inveterate enemy.

Speeches for Social Occasions.

A light touch is necessary while the digestive organs are functioning, and a good story, if relevant and brief, is a help.

Adulation of guests should be based on their work rather than on their personal attributes to avoid embarrassment.

When opening bazaars etc., speakers are usually expected to speak for at least five minutes, so points, jotted down and memorized, are recommended to suggest new trains of thought. If this is not done it is often difficult to fill in the allotted time, as the mind will only suggest getting the main task over as quickly as possible.

Points are a great help even for informal speeches and the effect is just as spontaneous if they are memorized.

Demonstrations.

Lectures with demonstrations are easy as the speaker's hands are occupied. It is better to stop speaking when the attention of the audience is focused on the demonstration, and then return to the lecture by repeating the point which the demonstration is intended to illustrate.

If articles are handed round at the request of the lecturer, it is better to do this after the speech, as anything which distracts the audience tends to disturb the speakers. Speakers themselves wishing to pass anything round should make a break in their speech for this purpose.

Appendix

Great Speeches and their Lessons

The writing of this Appendix is a concession to my creative mind, which has become restive under the lengthy spell of control by reason and logic which was necessary for the compiling of a simple text book on special training. Just as one's fingers develop writers' cramp as a protest, so one's free mind demands release from the irksome shackles, and I turn with relief from routine work to the pleasant and stimulating study of famous oratory.

Conclusions reached are purely individual, as they must be in the case of any reader who studies great speeches from his own angle of thought, and I hope it will not be deemed impertinent on my part to record impressions. Personal opinions require neither agreement nor criticism, though doubtless the former would be comforting and the latter stimulating.

My object in doing this is threefold, firstly purely selfish enjoyment, secondly that my conclusions may prove of passing interest to readers and lastly the desire to encourage others to extract valuable lessons from similar study, and to help them by providing a starting point, though doubtless their conclusions would be very different from mine, and possibly far sounder.

Lessons I have learnt are as follows, the first two being of outstanding importance, the others merely matters of interest.

1. That fear of the power of free speech has led to its suppression through the ages, rather than to its development, control, and use, as in the case of mechanical power.

2. That insincerity and man-made barriers dissolved the natural partnership between the free mind and the natural voice, the mind turning more and more to the medium of the pen for expression, while oratory became the cherished child of the elocutionist and the voice producer.

3. That famous speeches can be roughly classified in three groups:

 1. Constructive speeches.
 2. Emotional speeches.
 3. Popular speeches.

All good speeches are constructive and emotional, the classification being based on the predominant note – constructive and emotional are sincere thought naturally expressed, but popular speeches are gems of thought, sometimes genuine and sometimes imitation, presented in an artificial setting suited to the fashions of the period.

4. That constructive speeches which have moulded history were not so much original thoughts as original interpretations of the burning questions of the day. They were often a composite picture of the co-operative thought from many minds, with the speaker crystallizing and expressing the inarticulate thoughts of the masses. Mutual agreement on the central theme was the electric current between the speaker and the audience, which ignited sparks of interest and enthusiasm. Such sparks lit fires in hitherto unreceptive minds, fires which spread with amazing rapidity because they were fed with the fuel of public opinion. The inspiration of such speeches was usually some fundamental truth recurring in later speeches, often after a lapse of centuries.

5. That individual styles were a reflection of the character and personality of the speaker and varied in each case, though all shared a warm understanding of human nature, which modern jargon would describe as a sound knowledge of psychology.

Here then, are my five conclusions, and the following are the reasons and some selections from the speeches which prompted them.

Suppression of Free Speech

Oratory was the chief medium of expression long before speeches were recorded, but its power was never feared or realized, because it was used by those in authority for their own ends, or to support and strengthen popular beliefs, never to question them. Tribal leaders no doubt exhorted their followers to carry out their wishes, and the teachings of the Stoics and Spartans that character could only be developed through physical endurance was highly acceptable to the authorities, as it produced tough warriors. Speech was therefore looked on as a powerful and natural medium for moulding public opinion. The famous speeches of Pericles were typical of the accepted opinions of the day, and it was not until the spread of education that the potential power of speech was revealed. Plato and his disciples exploited this power and made Athens the cultural centre of the world, but their method of exploring individual minds, extracting revolutionary thoughts which dared to question accepted beliefs, and exchanging views by means of discussion groups, were sadly disturbing to the authorities, and started the train of persecution which has followed all speakers who dared to express freely and fearlessly unorthodox views. Socrates was executed for godlessness, Demosthenes took poison to escape another death, Cicero had his throat cut, Christ was crucified, the early Christians were thrown to the lions, and all through history those who used natural speech to express free thought were burned, tortured, and persecuted. Church and State were the great authorities, so heresy and treason were made the chief crimes in order that all challengers to those authorities might be speedily removed. As recently as the seventeenth century, John Bunyan was imprisoned for twelve years for protesting against the established State Church.

With the advance of civilization, more humane methods were introduced to achieve the same ends, and oratory was only encouraged in clerics, politicians, and lawyers, who spoke to selected audiences. Free speech was stifled by innumerable laws, its power weakened by insincerity, the deadliest enemy of true oratory, and ideas were directed into the safer channels of the pen and the printing press, where they could be censored and control-led, and writers discredited, and their ideas smothered before they could be fairly discussed. We are now reap-ing a harvest of dragons' teeth as a result of stifling individual thought and its free expression through dynamic speech. If the challenge to the written word is not met, Nature will reply with even more frustrations, inhibitions, and misery. Any authority that, through its educational system, can stifle free speech and produce mass minds which shirk individual responsibility, are presenting dictators with the key to power.

The most superficial study of the history of oratory, brings home the tragedy of the severing of the natural partnership of the creative mind and the voice, but there are hopeful signs that the wheel has turned full circle and that thinking people are returning to the wisdom of the Greeks, by means of Discussion Groups and the free inter-change of ideas.

The word Discussion comes from the Greek word dialective, but we must follow their methods and have trusted leaders, like Plato and Socrates, men of brilliant intellects and noble characters, who worshipped beauty, truth, and love, and whose aim was true education. They co-ordinated individual thought, eliminated personal prejudice and ignorance, and reached constructive con-clusions by means of tolerant, free, discussion.

We must go further than they went and relate our conclusions to our way of life, which they certainly did not, as their noble thoughts were remote from the barbarous methods practised in many phases of the national administration.

Demosthenes, when on trial for his oratory, defending himself against his rival orator Æschines in 330 B.C. gives us the following picture of the true functions of speech.

THE ORATION ON THE CROWN

(Delivered at Athens, 330 B.C. in Defence of Ktesiphon – from the Translation of Kennedy.)

"On what occasions ought an orator and statesman to be vehement? Where any of the commonwealth's main interests are in jeopardy, and he is opposed to the adversaries of the people. Those are the occasions for a generous and brave citizen.

"I should conclude, Æschines, that you undertook this cause to exhibit your eloquence and strength of lungs, not to obtain satisfaction for any wrong. But it is not the language of an orator, Æschines, that has any value, nor yet the tone of his voice, but his adopting the same views with the people, and his hating and loving the same persons that his country does. He that is thus minded will say everything with loyal intention; he that courts persons from whom the commonwealth apprehends danger to herself rides not on the same anchorage with the people, and therefore has not the same expectation of safety.

"And who is it that deceives the state? Surely the man who speaks not what he thinks. On whom does the crier pronounce a curse? Surely on such a man. What greater crime can an orator be charged with than that his opinions and his language are not the same? Such is found to be your character. And yet you open your mouth and dare to look these men in the face!"

Inspiration can surely be drawn from such a description of the power of speech, coupled with the tragic lesson of its suppression and debasement, which should call forth a determination to revive and use such power for good ends.

Let us now turn to a brief study of various types of famous speech such as – constructive, emotional, and popular.

Constructive Speeches.

The speeches from which I drew my conclusion regarding constructive speeches were (a) the speech of Pericles in 451 B.C. and (b) the Gettysburg Speech of Abraham Lincoln, delivered 2,000 years later, and both are reproduced below.

ON THE CAUSES OF ATHENIAN GREATNESS

(Extracts from an Oration delivered by Pericles at the Public Funeral of the Athenian Soldiers killed in the First Year of the Peloponnesian War, 431 B.C.).

"We are happy in a form of government which cannot envy the laws of our neighbours – for it hath served as a model to others, but is original at Athens. And this our form, as committed not to the few, but to the whole body of the people, is called a democracy. How different soever in a private capacity, we all enjoy the same general equality our laws are fitted to preserve; and superior honours just as we excel. The public administration is not confined to a particular family, but is attainable only by merit. Poverty is not a hindrance, since whoever is able to serve his country meets with no obstacle to preferment from his first obscurity. The offices of the State we go through without obstructions from one another; and live together in the mutual endearments of private life without suspicions; not angry with a neighbour for following the bent of his own humour, nor putting on that countenance of discontent, which pains thought it cannot punish – so that in private life we converse without diffidence or damage, while we dare not on any account offend against the public, through the reverence we bear to the magistrates and the laws, chiefly to those enacted for redress of the injured, and to those unwritten, a breach of which is thought a disgrace. Our laws have further provided for the mind most frequent intermissions of care, by the appointment of public recreations and sacrifices throughout the year, elegantly performed with a peculiar pomp, the daily delight of which is a charm that puts melanchology to flight. The grandeur of this our Athens causeth the produce of the whole earth to be imported here, by which we reap a familiar enjoyment, not more of the delicacies of our own growth than of those of other nations.

"In our manner of living we show an elegance tempered with frugality, and we cultivate philosophy without enervating the mind. We display our wealth in the season of beneficence and not in the vanity of discourse. A confession of poverty is disgrace to no man, no effort to avoid it is disgrace indeed. There is visible in the same persons an attention to their own private concerns and those of the public; and in others engaged in the labours of life there is a competent skill in the affairs of government. For we are the only people who think him that does not meddle in State affairs, not indolent, but good for nothing. And yet we pass the soundest judgements, and are quick at catching the right apprehensions of things, not thinking that words are prejudicial to actions, but rather the not being duly prepared by previous debate before we are obliged to proceed to the execution. Herein consists our distinguishing excellence, that in the hour of action we show the greatest courage, and yet debate beforehand the expediency of our measures. The courage of others is the result of ignorance; deliberation makes them cowards. And those undoubtedly must be owned to have the greatest soul, who, most acutely sensible of the miseries of war and the sweets of peace, are not hence in the least deterred from facing danger.

"In acts of beneficence, further we differ from the many. We preserve friends not by receiving, but by conferring, obligations. For he who does a kindness hath the advantage over him who, by the law of gratitude, becomes a debtor to his benefactor. The person obliged is compelled to act the more insipid part, conscious that a return of kindness is merely a payment and not an obligation. And we alone are splendidly beneficent to others, not so much from interested motives, as for the credit of pure liberality. I shall sum up what yet remains by only adding that our Athens in general is the school of Greece; and that every single Athenian amongst us is excellently formed, by his personal qualification, for all the various scenes of active life, acting with a most graceful demeanour and a most ready habit of dispatch.

"As for you, who now survive them, it is your business to pray for a better fate, but to think it your duty also to preserve the same spirit and warmth of courage against your enemies; not judging of the expediency of this from a mere harangue, where any man indulging a flow of words may tell you, what you yourselves know as well as he, how many advantages there are in fighting valiantly against your enemies, but, rather, making the daily-increasing grandeur of this community the object of your thoughts, and growing quite enamoured of it. And when it really appears great to your apprehensions, think again that this grandeur was acquired by brave and valiant men; by men who knew their duty, and in the moments of action were sensible of shame; who, whenever their attempts were unsuccessful, thought it dishonour their country should stand in need of anything their valour could do for it, and so made it the most glorious present. Bestowing thus their lives on the public, they have every one received a praise that will never decay, a sepulchre that will always be most illustrious – not that in which their bones lie mouldering, but that in which their frame is preserved – to be on every occasion, when honour is the employ of either word or act, eternally remembered."

This speech is also a good example of the recurrence of great ideas in history. Compare it with Abraham Lincoln's Gettysburg speech delivered nearly two thousand years later.

ADDRESS AT THE DEDICATION OF THE NATIONAL CEMETERY AT GETTYSBURG

Abraham Lincoln, *November* 19*th,* 1863.

"Fourscore and seven years ago our fathers brought forth upon this continent a new nation, conceived in liberty, and dedicated to the proposition that all men are created equal.

"Now we are engaged in a great civil war, testing whether that nation, or any nation so conceived and so dedicated, can long endure. We are met on a great portion of that field, as a final resting-place for those who here gave their lives that that nation might live. It is altogether fitting and proper that we should do this.

"But in a larger sense we cannot dedicate, we cannot consecrate, we cannot hallow this ground. The brave men, living and dead, who struggled here, have consecrated it far above our power to add or detract. The world will little note nor long remember what we say here, but it can never forget what they did here.

It is for us, the living, rather, to be dedicated here to the unfinished work which they who fought here have thus far so nobly advanced. It is rather for us to be here dedicated to the great task remaining before us; that from these honoured dead we take increased devotion to that cause for which they gave the last full measure of devotion; that we here highly resolve that these dead shall not have died in vain; that this nation, under God, shall have a new birth of freedom; and that government of the people, by the people, and for the people, shall not perish from the earth."

The circumstances in both cases were similar and therefore produced the same thoughts which accounts for the parallel lines on which the speeches were developed. There was tense emotion after a war, tribute to the fallen and a determination to justify their sacrifice, the vision of a people's world to comfort and inspire the masses who are the chief sufferers in every war, and an appeal to individual effort and responsibility. Had this noble conception of democracy been studied and followed, it would not be the mirage to which we pay lip service to-day, but both Pericles and Lincoln visualized responsible individuals, inspired by love of country and high ideals, and until we return to these standards such speeches seem singularly out of place.

Emotional Speeches

Speeches which have survived by the intensity of their emotional appeal were of two kinds. Some were delivered by men of great intellect, who balanced emotion with reason, and transmitted through their command of language a vivid, accurate, and appealing reproduction of the clear picture in their own minds. Others were of the volcanic type, a spontaneous eruption of great ideas, glowing with personal conviction, built up on superb mastery of words, noble phrases, or, stinging, searing words, as occasion demanded, embellished by appropriate gestures, and inflections, and depending more on emotional than reasoned appeal. Many of them were outstanding examples of moral courage which never paused to count the cost.

The following are illustrations of vivid picture painting.

(a) Emerson on the death of Lincoln.

(b) Randall Davidson on the Congo atrocities.

Emerson was better known as an essayist, but speeches often illuminate character more vividly than writings. A study of famous people should always include their speeches as well as their writings and biographies, if a true picture is to be formed.

Here you get the brevity of the writer, the eloquence of the thinker, and the perfect transmission of his mind picture of a human and rugged Lincoln.

THE GREATNESS OF A PLAIN AMERICAN

(Delivered at Concord, Massachusetts, on the Occasion of the Funeral Services in Honour of Mr. Lincoln, 1865).

"We meet under the gloom of a calamity which darkens down over the minds of good men in all civilized society, as the fearful tidings travel over sea, over land, from country to country, like the shadow of an uncalculated eclipse over the planet. Old as history is, and manifold as are its tragedies, I doubt if any death has caused so much pain to mankind as this has caused, or will cause on its announcement; and this not so much because nations are by modern arts brought so closely together, as because of the mysterious hopes and fears which, in the present day, are connected with the name and institutions of America. In this country, on Saturday, every one was struck dumb, and saw, at first, only deep below deep, as he meditated on the ghastly blow. And, perhaps, at this hour, when the coffin which contains the dust of the President sets forward on its long march through mourning States, on its way to his home in Illinois, we might well be silent, and suffer the awful voices of the time to thunder to us. Yes, but that first despair was brief; the man was not so to be mourned. He was the most active and hopeful of men and his work had not perished, but acclamations of praise for the task he had accomplished burst out into a song of triumph, which even tears for his death cannot keep down. The

President stood before us a man of the people. He was thoroughly American, had never crossed the sea, had never been spoiled by English insularity or French dissipation; a quiet, native, aboriginal man, as an acorn from the oak; no aping of foreigners, no frivolous accomplishments; Kentuckian born, working on a farm, a flatboatman, a captain in the Blackhawk War, a country lawyer, a representative in the rural legislature of Illinois – on such modest foundations the broad structure of his fame was laid. How slowly, and yet happily prepared steps, he came to his place! All of us remember – it is only a history of five or six years – the surprise and disappointment of the country at his first nomination at Chicago. Mr. Seward, then in the culmination of his good fame, was the favourite of the Eastern States. And when the new and comparatively unknown name of Lincoln was announced (notwithstanding the report of the acclamations of that convention) we heard the result coldly and sadly. It seemed too rash, on a purely local reputation, to build so grave a trust, in such anxious times; and men naturally talked of the chances in politics as incalculable. But it turned out not to be chance. The profound good opinion which the people of Illinois and of the West had conceived of him, and which they had imparted to their colleagues, that they also might justify themselves to their constituents at home, was not rash, though they did not begin to know the richness of his worth. A plain man of the people, an extraordinary fortune attended him. Lord Bacon says: 'Manifest virtues procure reputation; occult ones fortune.' He offered no shining qualities at the first encounter; he did not offend by superiority. He had a face and manner which disarmed suspicion, which inspired confidence, which confirmed good will. He was a man without vices. He had a strong sense of duty which it was very easy for him to obey. Then he had what farmers call a long head; was excellent in working out the sum for himself, in arguing his case and convincing you fairly and firmly. Then it turned out that he was a greater worker and that, having prodigious faculty of performance, he worked easily. A good worker is so rare; everybody has some one disabling quality. But this man was found to the very core, cheerful, persistent, all right for labour, and he liked nothing so well. Then he had a vast good nature, which made him tolerant and accessible to all; fairminded, leaning to the claim of the petitioner, affable and not sensible to the affliction which the innumerable visits paid him, when President, would have brought to anyone else. And how his good nature became a noble humanity in many a tragic case which events of war brought to him, everyone will remember, with what increasing tenderness he dealt when a whole race was on his compassion. The poor negro said of him on an impressive occasion, 'Massa Linkum am eberywhere'. Then his broad good humour, running easily into jocular talk, in which he delighted and in which he excelled, was a rich gift to this wise man. It enabled him to keep his secret, to meet every kind of man and every rank in society, to take off the edge of the severest decisions to mask his own purpose and sound his companions, and to catch with true instinct the temper of each company he addressed. And, more than all that, such good nature is to a man of severe labour, in anxious and exhausting crises, the natural restorative, good as sleep, and is the protection of the overdriven brain against rancour and insanity. He is the author of a multitude of good sayings, so disguised as pleasantries that it is certain that they had no reputation at first but as jests; and only later, by the acceptance and adoption they find in the mouths of millions, turn out to be the wisdom of the hour. I am sure if this man had ruled in a period of less facility of printing, he would have become mythological in a few years, like Æsop or Pilpay, or one of the Seven Wise Masters, by his fables and proverbs. But the weight and penetration of many passages in his letters, messages, and speeches, hidden now by the very closeness of their application to the moment, are destined hereafter to wide fame. What pregnant definitions; what unerring common sense; what foresight; and on great occasions, what lofty and more than natural, what human tone! His occupying the chair of State was a triumph of the good sense of mankind and of the public confidence. This middle class country has got a middle class President at last. Yes, in manners, sympathy, but not in powers, for his powers were superior. His mind mastered the problem of the day; and, as the problem grew, so did his comprehension of it. Rarely was a man so fitted to the event. In the midst of fears and jealousies, in the babel of counsels and parties, this man wrought incessantly with all his might and all his honesty, labouring to find what the people wanted, and how to obtain that. It cannot be said there is any exaggeration of his worth. If ever a man was fairly tested, he was. There was no lack of resistance, nor of slander, nor of ridicule. The times have allowed no State secrets; the nation has been in such a ferment, such multitudes had to be entrusted, that no secret could be kept. Every door was ajar, and we all knew what befell. Then what an occasion was the whirlwind of the war! Here was place for no public magistrate, no fairweather sailor; the new pilot was hurried to the helm in a tornado. In four years, the four years of battle days, his endurance, his fertility of recourses, his magnanimity, were sorely tried and never found wanting. There, by his courage, his justice, his even temper his fertile counsel, his humanity, he stood, an heroic figure in the centre of an heroic epoch. He is the true history of the American people in his time. Step by step, he walked, before them, slow with their slowness, quickening his march by theirs; the true representative of this continent; an entirely public man; father of his country, the pulse of twenty millions throbbing in his heart, the though of their minds articulated by his tongue, Adam Smith remarks that the axe which in Houbraken's portraits of British kings and worthies is engraved under those who have suffered at the block adds a certain lofty charm to the picture. And who does not see, even in this tragedy so recent, how fast the terror and ruin of the massacre are already burning into glory around the victim? Far happier this fate than to have lived to be wished away, to have watched the decay of his own faculties; to have seen – perhaps even he – the proverbial ingratitude of statesmen; to have seen mean men preferred. Had he not lived long enough to keep the greatest promise that ever man made to his fellow-men – the practical abolition of slavery? He had seen Tennessee, Missouri, and Maryland emancipate their slaves. He had seen Savannah, Charleston, and Richmond surrendered; had seen the main army of the Rebellion lay down its arms. He had conquered the public opinion of Canada, England, and France. Only Washington can compare with him in fortune. And what if it should turn out, in the unfolding of the web, that he had reached the term; that this heroic deliverer could no longer serve us; that the rebellion had touched its natural conclusion, and what remained to be done required new and uncommitted hands – a new spirit born out of the ashes of the war; and that Heaven, wishing to show the world a completed benefactor, shall make him serve his country even more by his death than his life. Nations, like kings, are not good by facility and complaisance. 'The kindness of kings consists in justice and strength.' Easy good nature has been the dangerous foible of the Republic, and it was necessary that its enemies should outrage it, and drive us to unwonted firmness, to secure the salvation of this country in the next ages."

The second illustration of vivid colouring is the speech of Randall Davidson, long revered as Archbishop of Canterbury, an outstanding example of making facts live in the minds of audiences by a series of simple pictures, with illustrations readily grasped by all.

"HIDEOUS OUTRAGES" OF SUBJUGATION

(From the Primate's Speech at a Meeting in Albert Hall, London, held November 19th, 1909, to Protest Against Belgian Methods of Exploitation in the Congo Free State).

"One plain fact. Do people realize the size of the region which we commonly call the Congo? Compare it with regions we know better. Draw a straight line from Edinburgh to Constantinople. Draw another from St. Petersburg to Rome. Draw another from Bordeaux to Warsaw. The area you cross and cover will be less than the area which we describe as the Congo. Now, what has really happened as regards that great tract of the world's surface? I think we see it best if we look successively at a few episodes – at what people sometimes call cameos – in the story. First picture – begin with some five and thirty years ago. Lovett Cameron and Henry Stanley in the seventies startled the world by their revelation, their unveiling of the land which had been practically unknown, its gigantic range of fertile provinces, with more than 5,000 miles of navigable waterway giving access to its varied wealth, with peoples innumerable, rude and simple, but full of eagerness, intelligence, and promise. It was, as Stanley said, 'like looking in the bright face of a little child and wondering where unto this will grow'. He threw himself with enthusiasm into their praises and their hopes, and he drew people along with him every day. Let anyone read the chapter called 'The Kernel of the Argument' in the second volume of his great book on the Congo if he would know what high ground there was for the buoyant optimism that Stanley everywhere inspired ...

"In his Guildhall speech ten days ago the Prime Minister summed up the facts in these words, weighty and unanswerable: 'The conditions on which the Congo Free State was founded have not only never been fulfilled; they have been continuously and habitually violated. The country has been closed to trade, the inhabitants have been deprived of customary rights, and subjected to a system of forced labour; and their condition, going steadily from bad to worse, has become the truly appalling condition which is described, not by sensational reporters, not by hysterical (as some people call them!) – hysterical missionaries, but in a long series of Parliamentary papers, reports from our own consuls, and in the investigation by Belgium itself through a commission appointed a few years ago.'

"The hideous outrages which have been recorded with quiet and unfaltering persistence by those competent and responsible observers are ghastly beyond all words. But, friends, they are not themselves the foundation evil. If we could be sure tomorrow that they had come to an end, the evil would not therefore be removed. The evil lies in the fact that the land is governed, or, rather, utilized, not for the good of the inhabitants, but for the gain or profit of its so-called owners in Europe. The outrages done by the native soldiers and petty agents are simply due to the necessities, imposed on them by their European masters, of enforcing the production of the rubber which becomes scarcer week by week. That will be brought out for you by others. I will not dwell upon it now. The picture – my fourth picture – is simply and sadly that of a great land whereon high hopes were set, so degraded, neglected, and oppressed that I suppose it would now take years of wise and tender government even at the best to bring it back again, up again, to the level of what was called its barbarous condition when Stanley unveiled it thirty or forty years ago. And for that, once more, England is in part responsible. Will spokesmen tonight be wrong in asking your resolve with acclamation that, if these things are to go on, England dare not, and will not hold her tongue?"

Another outstanding example of this type of speech is William Pitt's plea for the immediate abolition of slavery made to Parliament in 1792. His conviction of the rightness of his cause, his insistence on the right of every individual to be free and happy and the clever way in which he assumed the assent of his listeners, are all points to note.

VOLCANIC SPEECHES

The choice of volcanic speeches is wide. I have chosen Victor Hugo's speech at the planting of the Liberty Tree in Paris 1848, because it shows how his strong religious views burst through what was doubtless intended to be a political speech.

THE LIBERTY TREE IN PARIS

(Delivered at the Planting of the Liberty Tree in the Place des Vosges 1848.)

"It is with joy that I yield to the call of my fellow-citizens, and come to hail in their midsts the hopes of emancipation, or order, and of peace which will germinate, blend with the roots of this tree of Liberty.

"What a true and Beautiful symbol for Liberty is this tree! Liberty has its roots in the hearts of the people, as the tree in the heart of the earth; like the tree it raises and spreads its branches to heaven; like the tree it is ceaseless in its growth, and it covers generations with its shade!

"The first tree of Liberty was planted eighteen hundred years ago by God himself on Golgotha! The first tree of Liberty was that cross on which Jesus Christ was offered a sacrifice, for the liberty, equality, and fraternity of the human race!

"The significance of this tree has not changed in eighteen centuries! Only let us not forget that with new times are new duties. The revolution which our fathers made sixty years ago was great by war; the revolution which you make today should be great by peace. The first destroyed; the second should organize! The work of organization is the necessary complement to the work of destruction. It is that which connects 1848 intimately to 1789. To establish, to create, to produce, to pacify; to satisfy all rights, to develop all the grand instincts of man, to provide for all the needs of society – this is the task of the future. And in the times in which we live, the future comes quickly!

"One can almost say the future is but tomorrow! It commences today! To the task then! To the task, workers with hands; workers with intelligence; you who hear me, you who surround me! Complete this great work of the fraternal organisation of all peoples, leading to the same object, attached to the same idea, and living with the same heart. Let us all be men of good will, let us spare neither our toil nor our sweat. Let us spread among all the peoples who surround us and over the whole world sympathy, charity, and fraternity.

"For three centuries the world has imitated France; for three centuries France has been the first of nations. And do you know what that means – 'the first of nations'? It means the greatest, it should also mean the best. My friends, my brothers, my fellow-citizens, let us establish throughout the whole world, by the grandeur of our example, the empire of our ideas! That each nation may be happy and proud to resemble France!

"Let us unite, then, in one common thought, and join with me in the cry: 'Hail to Universal Liberty! All hail to the Universal Republic'!"

JUDICIAL SPEECHES

Great judicial speeches were triumphs of reasoned argument, notably for their clear-cut marshalling of fact. Emotion was used sparingly and usually reserved for the appeal to the jury at the end. A good example is Edmund Burke's conclusion at the impeachment of Warren Hastings in 1788 showing his masterly appeal to the fair-mindedness of the jury, his concise charges, and the way in which the natural eloquence for which he was noted was subordinated to serve his judicial purpose.

"Do we want a tribunal? My lords, no example of antiquity, nothing in the modern world, nothing in the range of human imagination, can supply us with a tribunal like this. My lords, here we see virtually in the mind's eye that sacred majesty of the Crown, under whose authority you sit, and whose power you exercise. We see in that invisible authority, what we all feel in reality and life, the beneficent powers and protecting justice of his Majesty. We have here the heir apparent to the Crown, such as the fond wishes of the people of England wish an heir apparent of the Crown to be. We have here all the branches of the royal family in a situation between majesty and subjection, between the sovereign and the subject, offering a pledge in that situation for the support of the rights of the Crown and the liberties of the people, both which extremities they touch. My lords, we have a great hereditary peerage here; those, who have their own honour, the honour of their ancestors, and of their posterity, to guard, and who will justify, as they have always justified, that provision in the Constitution by which justice is made an hereditary office. My lords, we have here a new nobility, who have risen and exalted themselves by various merits, by great military services which have extended the fame of this country from the rising to the setting sun. We have those, who by various civil merits and various civil talents have been exalted to a situation, which they well deserve, and in which they will justify the favour of their sovereign and the good opinion of their fellow-subjects, and make them rejoice to see those virtuous characters, that were the other day upon a level with them, now exalted above them in rank, but feeling with them in sympathy what they felt in common with them before. We have persons exalted from the practice of the law, from the place in which they administered high, though subordinate, justice, to a seat here, to enlighten with their knowledge and to strengthen with their votes those principles which have distinguished the courts in which they have presided.

"My lords, you have also here the lights of our religion; you have the bishops of England. My lords, you have the true image of the primitive church in its ancient form, in its ancient ordinances, purified from the superstitions and the vices which a long succession of ages will bring upon the best institutions. You have the representatives of that religion which says that their God is love, that the very vital spirit of their institution is charity – a religion, which so much hates oppression, that when the God whom we adore appeared in human form, he did not appear in a form of greatness and majesty, but in sympathy with the lowest of the people, and thereby made it a firm and ruling principle that their welfare was the object of all government, since the person, who was the Master of Nature, chose to appear Himself in a subordinate situation. These are the considerations which influence them, which animate them, and will animate them against all oppression, knowing that He who is called first among them and first among us all, both of the flock that is fed and of those who feed it, made Himself the servant of all.'

"My lords, these are the securities which we have in

all the constituent parts of the body of this House. We know them, we reckon, we rest upon them, and commit safely the interests of India and of humanity into your hands. Therefore, it is with confidence, that, ordered by the Commons,

"I impeach Warren Hastings, Esquire, of high crimes and misdemeanours.

"I impeach him in the name of the Commons of Great Britain in Parliament assembled, whose parliamentary trust he has betrayed.

"I impeach him in the name of all the Commons of Great Britain, whose national character he has dishonoured.

"I impeach him in the name of the people of India, whose laws, rights, and liberties he has subverted; whose properties he has destroyed; whose country he has laid waste and desolate.

"I impeach him in the name, and by virtue, of those eternal laws of justice which he has violated.

"I impeach him in the name of human nature itself, which he has cruelly outraged, injured, and oppressed in both sexes, in every age, rank, situation, and condition of life."

POLITICAL SPEECHES

Political speeches reached their zenith with the growth of political parties in the eighteenth and nineteenth centuries and can best be studied by taking two of the great oratorical giants such as William Pitt and Charles Fox, or Disraeli and Gladstone and noting the battle of ideas, the play of great intellects and the verbal fireworks, sharpened, but never debased, by personal antagonism. Gladstone's tribute to Disraeli was a good example of this pleasant feature of English political life. Many political speeches were in the nature of crusades, such as the passionate love of Empire of Joseph Chamberlain and the eloquence of Keir Hardie on behalf of the working man. Others were statesmanlike in their breadth and vision such as Salisbury, Grey, and Winston Churchill, while speakers like Lloyd George had an uncanny knack of reproducing the unspoken thoughts of the ordinary people in colourful language.

POPULAR SPEECHES

Popular speeches are the type presented in the style of the period – when the artistry of the language and the composition of the speeches are designed to attract listeners.

The conversational method of the Athenians was suited to the graceful toying with ideals. Cicero on the other hand exemplified the Roman ideal of perfection in detail, and when the turbulence of revolutionary ideas was suppressed, attention was focused on style, and the poetry of Cicero's speeches, with his love of words and finely modelled prose, became accepted as the standards of good oratory for hundreds of years.

Bunyan typified the short, concise, blunt, but powerful picture-painting method of the English orators, who believed in calling a spade a spade, and his pictures of Heaven and Hell were amazingly realistic.

The Elizabethan age produced many such orators, the Cromwellian period was noted for severe puritanical speeches and the flamboyant and florid style in vogue sixty years ago was typical of the over-ornamentation of the Victorian age.

The twentieth century with its labour-saving inventions, its cheap Press and ready-made opinions, has made mental concentration, which alone produces the individual thought of which great speeches are made, unnecessary and almost impossible for the masses, with the result that oratory has reached its lowest ebb, and the pre-digested radio talk, the relating of personal experiences, and the fireside chat is the mode of the moment. The turn of the tide is due, however, and the future may see a rising standard, with the re-birth of individual responsibility, insistence on more general use of the immense, untapped source of power contained in sincere, constructive thought, expressed through free unfettered speech.

To sum up the lessons gleaned from the study of famous speeches which have outlived their creators, they were the products of brilliant intellects, proving that knowledge is the background and that the mind directs the voice; the initial approach was through emotion to reason, the mastery of words and phrasing produced the beauty and the character of the speaker, lit up the meaning, while the force of conviction drove home the points. To succeed as a speaker requires knowledge, feeling, sincerity, skill in the use of words, and a passionate belief in the power of speech which will enable us to reach a goal which seems far off to many at the moment. We have no means of judging the part played by the voice in the delivery of these speeches, but the fact that read speeches can inspire by the force of ideas and language, proves beyond doubt that the mind is the controlling force in effective speech, and that science of the mind should precede the art of delivery in any reliable method of speech.